# Lake District Place-Names

by
Robert Gambles

Dalesman Books
1985

The Dalesman Publishing Company Ltd.
Clapham, Via Lancaster, LA2 8EB

First published 1980
Second edition 1985

ISBN: 0 85206 814 X

By the same author:
**MAN IN LAKELAND**
**LAKELAND VALLEYS**

Phototypeset, printed and bound by Galava Printing Company Ltd., Nelson, Lancs.

# Contents

The illustrations are by A. Wainwright who generously gave his permission for their use.

**Elterwater—the lake of the swans** (see page 15)

# Preface

THE study of place-names is properly a matter for the scholar and the linguistic expert: the non-specialist who ventures here enters a minefield and is fortunate indeed to avoid the many dangers of falling into error and misinterpretation which beset him. Even so, it is a subject which holds a strange fascination for very many people, and in my years of lecturing and discussion on the history of the Lake District I have been asked more questions on this topic than on any other. This little book is an attempt to satisfy this commendable curiosity in a manner which combines simplicity in presentation with the minimum of linguistic information necessary for an intelligent understanding of each name. I am very much aware that it may seem over-simplified to the specialist, but my purpose is to bring some of the fruits of long and intense academic work by a number of distinguished experts to those who, understandably, feel overwhelmed by the daunting volumes of linguistic studies and by the professional expertise of those who write them.

I gladly acknowledge my own indebtedness to these authorities and, in particular, to the following works which I have made the basis of my own studies in the compilation of this short guide:

*The Place-names of Cumberland:* Volumes XX, XXI, XXII in the publications of the English Place-name Society (Cambridge 1950-52).

*The Place-names of Westmorland:* Volume XLII in the same series (Cambridge 1967).

A.H. Smith—*English Place-name Elements:* Volume XXV and XXVI in the same series (Cambridge 1956).

E. Ekwall—*The Oxford Dictionary of English Place-names* (Oxford 1967).

E. Ekwall—*English River-names* (Oxford 1928).

E. Ekwall—*Scandinavians and Celts in the North West of England* (Lund 1918).

W.J. Sedgefield—*The Place-names of Cumberland and Westmorland* (Manchester 1915).

H. Lindkvist—*Middle English Place-names of Scandinavian Origin* (Uppsala 1912).

David Mills—*The Place-names of Lancashire* (Batsford 1976).
*The Transactions of the Cumberland and Westmorland Antiquarian and Archaeological Society.*

I wish also to express my gratitude to Dr. David Mills of the University of Liverpool who gave so generously of his time in reading and discussing the typescript and to Professor Kenneth Cameron of the University of Nottingham who answered my questions with patience and authority and guided me firmly away from treacherous ground.

Robert Gambles

### Preface to Second Edition

The publication of a Second Edition has given an opportunity to make several amendments and corrections to the text where it seemed that recent studies or points of additional interest or clarification made this desirable.

Robert Gambles
Kendal 1985

**Skelwith Force, derived from 'Schelwath'—the noisy ford**
(see page 44)

# Introduction

PLACE-NAMES were once words used in everyday speech, words which described one particular spot and distinguished it clearly and unmistakeably from all other places in the immediate neighbourhood. The description might be no more than a simple identification of the man or family who lived there—so Finsthwaite was Finn's clearing—or it might refer to some natural feature—Ashness, the headland with the ash trees—or it might indicate a particular activity or function—Keswick, the cheese dairyfarm. Whatever the chosen description, it would leave no doubt within a small community of the precise location of the place referred to. It follows, therefore, that all place-names were used in spoken form long before they were first written down, and this transmission of the spoken words from generation to generation, perhaps for several hundred years, resulted in subtle changes which now present many problems for the place-name scholar, for whom the earliest written form of a name may itself be no more than a semi-phonetic spelling in a language no longer in use. Our knowledge of the languages spoken by the many peoples who have settled in Britain has greatly increased during the last half century and we are now able to attempt an explanation of most of the place-names which have survived and which we accept today in forms standardised by more than a hundred years of modern spelling and usage.

Place-name studies have much to offer the serious scholar. The linguist can learn something of the sounds and structure of ancient tongues and of the process by which our modern speech has emerged from the confusion of languages and dialects spoken by our ancestors; the geographer can trace the changing patterns of land use and settlement; the biologist can discover the animals and birds which frequented the countryside, and the botanist the plants and flowers; the historian can add to the evidence of his documents all the detail revealed by the 'history on the map', for place-names reflect the movement of peoples, their folklore and mythology, their religious beliefs, their political and military administration, their local customs and social institutions, and often their personal names, appearance and eccentricities. For all of us, specialist or not, place-names can be yet another fascinating source of information

7

about our remote forebears who first gave names to our farms, fields, cottages and hamlets, and to the lakes, rivers and woodlands by which they lived.

The first settlers in Cumbria were probably a British community which, perhaps six thousand years ago, lived in tiny villages along the western seaboard. We know little about them and it seems unlikely that their language has survived in any recognisable form. Some two thousand years later these same coastal settlements and also many more in the valleys of the rivers Kent and Eden (and even a few in the high fell-country) were occupied by families of Celts, the people whom the Romans found here towards the end of the first century A.D. The Roman legions left little mark on the place-names of this remote part of their empire: the once busy and important military fortresses and their bustling townships have been erased almost completely from the map. Who now would ask the way to Galava, Mediobogdum or Glannaventa? And yet the tongue of the conquered Celt has survived, for these people were the 'Cymri' who gave their name to 'Cumbria' itself and whose language 'Cumbric' was spoken here for centuries after the fall of Rome. It is their speech which has come down to us in such harmonious names as 'Blencathra', Glencoyne', Glenderamackin', and Penruddock'.

The Roman occupation was followed in the 5th and 6th centuries by the extensive colonisation of England by the Angles and Saxons, but they seem to have made little impact on the lands of the Cymri. Anglo-Saxons 'tuns', 'hams', 'ings' and 'leas' lie thick on the ground in many English counties, but in the highlands of Cumbria they are few and far between. The fertile valleys of Buttermere, Windermere and Grasmere appealed to these dairy-farming peoples seeking new pastures in pleasant places, but their influence is seen most of all in the western coastal plain, the broad vales of Kent and Eden and on the Solway Firth. The Romano-British tribes continued their precarious existence in the remoter valleys, in their craggy fortresses and in their windswept villages on the high moorlands. The days of prosperous co-existence with the Roman conqueror were over: the days of oblivion when the tide of Norsemen swept over their land were yet to come.

In the interlude, these descendants of the warlike Celts resisted Anglian pressure and for a time were successful—long enough for the missionaries of the Christian Church in Ireland to establish their religion in these northern districts of an otherwise heathen land. Little is known of their mission and much of their story is now overlaid with legend and embroidered folklore. Certainly a number of Cumbrian churches are dedicated to St. Kentigern (perhaps better known as St. Mungo), and local tradition in some parts clings closely to St. Ninian, St. Patrick and St. Martin. This is where place-names sometimes help to create and perpetuate historical traditions for which there is no other more reliable evidence. We can only be certain that while the rest of England awaited the arrival of Saint Augustine and his mission from Rome in 597, some of the peoples of Cumbria were already familiar with the teachings of the Christian Church.

In the 10th century, a new migration of peoples almost overwhelmed this misty civilisation and within a comparatively short time the language and landscape of Cumbria were transformed. The last vestiges of the British and Anglian cultures were swept aside, leaving only faint traces in a few recently erected stone crosses and a few surviving place-names.

It was now the turn of the Norsemen. These were not the plundering raiders who ravaged much of England and from whose fury a special Litany asked for God's protection, but farmers of Norse descent from Ireland and Western Scotland who came not to kill and destroy but to build new homes for their families in the mountain valleys of Lakeland and on the wide spaces of the fertile lowlands. Taking their Herdwick sheep with them, they penetrated deep into the heartland of the Lake District and with incredible labour they cleared the forest, the scrub and the Ice Age rubble which covered the valley floors. They built their homesteads, byres and barns, reared their stock and planted crops. They gave Norse names to the fells and crags, to the lakes, tarns and streams; to the high pastures where they built their summer shielings and to the valleys where they recreated a way of life such as their parents and grandparents had known in Norway—a way of life which persisted in Cumbria until well into the Middle Ages. Norse speech was used until the 13th century and even now still forms a significant part of Cumbrian dialect, while the predominance of Norse place-names in Lakeland is a permanent reminder of this last important colonisation, just one thousand years ago. How far Norse names replaced earlier British or Anglian names we may never know (for we cannot safely assume that the last arrival to give a place its name was also the first), but the abundance of Norse names leaves little doubt that as most of England succumbed to the Norman yoke, a thriving Scandinavian community flourished here in the North—and continued to do so for many years to come.

In our search for place-names we come across traces of the folk who came to make their homes in the Lake District. Whether we look for British names near Skiddaw and Ullswater, Anglian names in the lowland plains, or Norse names in the mountain valleys and the uplands, we should always remember that it was only a small number of men and women—perhaps no more than a few hundred families —who, by their unceasing labours, began the long and arduous process of creating out of the chaos of forest and waste that harmony between the work of Man and the work of Nature which, in the fullness of time, was to become Lakeland's unique attraction.

Knut Hamsun in his book *The Growth of the Soil* gives us a brief

**The Tottling Stone, Launchy Gill, owes its name to the Cumbrian dialect verb 'to tottle' meaning to be unsteady or liable to topple over** (see page 52)

glimpse into this remote pioneering past when he describes the end of one man's long and patient search for a place to settle in a strange and unknown land:

In the morning he sees before him a landscape of woodland and open grass; as he climbs down over the green fellside he catches a glimpse of the river far below and of a hare leaping over it at one bound. He is well-pleased that the river is no wider than just a single jump. A nesting grouse flies up suddenly from beneath his feet and hisses angrily at him, and again he observes that here are both animals and wildfowl—a useful point to bear in mind. He wanders over heather and bilberry and among the woodland flowers and ferns; here and there he stops to dig into the ground with his iron spike and he finds good soil in one place and peat in another, the loam of several thousand years of fallen leaves and decayed twigs and branches. He makes his decision: it is here that he will stay, here that he will settle down .... It had indeed been hard work to find just the right place; it was still a place without a name, but now it was his.

So a place-name was born and as the months passed by, he also gave names to the streams and the woodlands, the craggy landmarks and all the wild and uncharted places in the surrounding fells.

Later ages added their own small but distinctive contribution, reflecting the impact of the political and social changes which are part of the relentless historical progress of human societies. The Norman barons carved up the land after their final conquest of this last corner of their new domain, but they were largely content to hand over vast tracts of these rugged and uncouth territories to the religious Orders who had an eye and, indeed, a preference for such places, remote from the turmoil of the world and yet with promising economic resources. Much of the heart of Lakeland came into the hands of the great Norman Abbeys of Fountains and Furness, but for the most part the existing English and Norse place-names remained and only here and there do we find clear traces of monastic activities—their 'granges' (or granaries and outlying farms) in Borrowdale and Furness; their mining industry in 'Ore Gap'; their land development in 'Newlands'; perhaps their woollen industry in the numerous 'Tenter Howes'; and in such specific names as 'Monk Coniston', 'Monk Foss', 'Monks' Bridge' and 'Abbot's Ridding'. The sudden dissolution of the monastic foundations in the 16th century resulted in the appearance of new farms created out of parts of their estates: these are the 'grounds' which figure so prominently on the map of High Furness—'Roger Ground', 'Jackson Ground', 'Stephenson Ground' and many others.

The industrial thrust of more modern times based on the mining of metals, the quarrying of slate, charcoal burning and the abundant water power used in hundreds of mills has also left its mark in such names as 'Copperheap Bay', 'Slater Bridge', 'Coledale' and the many names indicating the existence of a 'forge' or 'mill'.

The locally, and sometimes the nationally, famous have occasionally left a place-name to mark their passing: Adelaide Hill, Birkett Fell, Belle Isle, Moses' Trod, Lanty's Tarn, Doctor's Bridge and Ritson Force. But on the map of Lakeland such 'new' names are few indeed. By far the great majority of names owe their origin to the peoples who first 'stubbed the waste' in the years before the Norman Conquest.

# Note on the Languages

THE place-names of Cumbria reflect the languages spoken by the different European peoples who came to live there. Most of them arrived, as we have seen, before the Norman Conquest, that is to say in the days before written records were commonly kept, and consequently the reconstruction of their languages is fraught with many difficulties which demand a scholarly appreciation of the structure of several now almost obsolete tongues and of the complex processes of change and development which a language can undergo. Scholars who have studied the place-names of the Lake District have delved long and deeply into the language of the ancient Britons and Celts, the ancestors of modern Welsh; into that of the Anglo-Saxons, whose language we call Old English; into that of the Norsemen, who spoke old Norse, the forerunner of modern Icelandic, Danish and Norwegian; and finally into that of the Norman-French who influenced the development of the English language during the Middle Ages.

It is impossible—and it would be inappropriate—to attempt to discuss here the many problems which are involved in the etymology of place-name study. In the planning of this brief guide for the general reader, the principal aim has been to present the material in a form which is both easily understood and consistent with accepted academic standards. One of the main difficulties is the fundamental difference in spelling conventions between the earlier languages and modern English. We find, for example, particularly in Old English and Old Norse, certain letters which are no longer in use. Fortunately, these can, fairly accurately, be represented by modern equivalents, and this has been done throughout this book.

The signs ð and þ, which in Old English and Old Norse represented the sound th' as in 'thin' and 'thus' are here given in modern form: for example the word 'thwaite' so commonly found in Lakeland place-names and derived from the Old Norse word 'þveit' is shown as 'thveit'. Certain 'o' sounds in Old Norse were represented by the sign 'ǫ'; this particular sound is not given any special distinction in the forms shown here.

Two important signs have been retained, however:
   i. The letter 'æ' in early languages is the equivalent of several of

12

the 'a' sounds and cannot be satisfactorily represented in any other way.

ii. The signs ‾ and ′ indicate the long vowel sound in Old English and Old Norse respectively and they are important guides to the later development of the words concerned.

Other points to bear in mind are:

i. There are no silent letters in the early languages: every letter represents a sound;

ii. Old English uses 'c', 'sc' and 'f' where modern English uses 'ch', 'sh', and 'v': for example O.E. cirice = church.

iii. Old English uses the letter 'c' and Old Norse uses the letter 'k' where modern English uses 'k' and 'ck' as well as 'c': for example O.E. blaec = black; O.N. bekkr = beck.

iv. Certain inflexions occur in the composition and development of place-names such as the possessive 's' as seen in names such as Finsthwaite, Hartsop and Brotherswater. These inflexions are not commented upon in each example as in most cases the technical point is evident from the explanation of the name as a whole.

v. Inversion Compounds: the Norse settlers in Cumbria who came from Ireland brought with them a feature of the Gaelic language not found in either Old English or Old Norse—the inversion compound. This involves an inversion of the usual order of words, and in place-names this often means that the word for 'farm', 'hill' or other natural feature is placed first and the descriptive adjective or the name of the owner is placed second. Examples of such inversion compounds are seen in 'Basebrown', 'Seat Sandal' and 'Starling Dodd'.

The following abbreviations have been used to indicate the language of origin of the place-name elements:

| | | |
|---|---|---|
| Br. | — | words of British or Celtic origin. |
| Gael. | — | Gaelic. |
| Welsh | — | words derived from the Old Welsh or Modern Welsh languages. |
| O.E. | — | Old English (spoken from about the 5th to the 11th century). |
| O.Dan. | — | Old Danish. |
| O.N. | — | Old Norse. |
| O.Fr. | — | Old French. |
| M.E. | — | Middle English (spoken from about the 12th to the 15th century). |
| dial. | — | words commonly used in Cumbrian or North Country dialect. |
| * | — | indicates a word not recorded but reconstructed by linguistic experts. |
| E.P.N.S.— | | English Place-name Society publications. |

# Plan of the Book

THE place-names included in this short guide have, for the most part, been selected from those found within the boundaries of the Lake District National Park. Approximately four hundred of the places most familiar to visitors have been chosen—only a very small fraction of the total number which is little short of 8,000 if one lists every wood, barn, beck and bridge and each one of the 28 Raven Crags. For a comprehensive record of almost every place-name in Cumbria the relevant volumes of the publications of the English Place-name Society should be consulted (see Preface, page 5).

To avoid too many cross-references in the text and to facilitate easy reference to any particular name, some information is duplicated as, for example, Rydal and Rydal Water, Shap and Shap Fell. To avoid frequent repetition in the text a glossary of all the elements which make up the place-names given in the book appears at the end. Here the more specific meaning of each element is indicated.

The analysis of each place-name varies according to the nature of the material included. Where appropriate a few details are given of special or local interest and the format is modified to accommodate this and other additional points of interest, but in most cases the main framework of each analysis is as follows:

   i. The modern name.
  ii. A brief explanation of its original meaning.
 iii. Brief details of its linguistic origin.
  iv. One example (or occasionally two examples) of an early form of the name, where this is available, to indicate its origin and development. In many cases no early forms are known. For example:

KESWICK: The cheese farm. O.E. cēse + O.E. wīc. Kesewic c. 1240, Chesewyk 1285. The 'K' at the beginning of the name is the result of Norse influence on an Old English word.

# The Lakes

**Bassenthwaite Lake:** The lake by Bastun's clearing. 'Bassen' is probably derived from a personal name, either O.E. Beahstan or a Norman-French nickname, Bastun, meaning 'a stick'. Bastun + O.N. thveit + (in modern times) 'Lake'. Bastunthwaite c.1170, Bastunwater c.1220.

**Brotherswater:** Popular legend derives this name from a story that two brothers were drowned in the lake but no details are known. The name may be derived from O.E. brōthor, brother, with the possessive 's' intruded; alternatively it may come from an O.N. personal name, Brothir + O.E. wæter = water. Brotherwater 1671, Broad Water 1777.

**Buttermere:** The lake by the dairy pastures (i.e. well-known for their butter). O.E. butere + O.E. mĕre. Butermere c.1230.

**Coniston Water:** The lake was formerly known as Thurston Water a name derived from the O.N. personal name Thursteinn + O.E. wæter. Turstiniwatra c.1160, Thurstainewater 1196. See Coniston—page 39.

**Crummock Water:** The lake of the crooked river. This seems to be linked with the derivation of the River Cocker which flows through the lake. See River Cocker—page 21. Br. crumbaco* = crooked + O.E. wæter. Crombocwater c.1307.

**Derwentwater:** The lake of the river which abounds in oak trees. 'Derwent' is a fairly common British river-name and seems to be derived from Br. derw*, an oak tree and derwentio*, abounding in oak trees. The same root is found also in the River Darent in Kent, the Dart in Devon, the Darwen in Lancashire and in the Yorkshire and Derbyshire Derwents. See River Derwent—page 21. Derewentwatre c.1240.

**Devoke Water:** This is probably derived from an Old Welsh or Old Irish word 'dubaco'* meaning 'the dark one'. Such a description might apply either to the dark appearance of the lake or possibly to a particular individual who lived near it. There are many ancient settlements on the moors around the lake. Duvokeswater c.1205.

**Elterwater:** The lake of the swans. O.N. elptar + O.E. wæter. Whooper swans still come to winter on the lake. Helterwatra c.1157.

Panorama from Castle Head over Derwentwater—the lake of the
river which abounds in oak trees

**Ennerdale Water:** This name means 'the lake in the valley of the River Ehen,' but before the 14th century the valley was known as Anenderdale or Anund's valley from an O.N. personal name. O.N. Anundar + O.N. dalr + O.E. wæter. (See River Ehen—page 22.) Anenderdale 1135, Eghnerdale 1321.

**Esthwaite Water:** The lake by the eastern clearing. O.N. ēast + O.N. thveit + O.E. wæter. Estwater 1537.

**Grasmere:** The lake with the grassy shores or the grassy lake. O.E. graes + O.E. mēre. Gresemere c.1240.

**Hawes Water:** Hafr's lake. 'Hafr' is an O.N. word for a he-goat, but here it is probably used as a nickname or even as a personal name. Havereswater 1199.

**Hayes Water:** Eithr's lake. Eithr is an Old Icelandic personal name and this seems to be the most likely origin of this place-name. An alternative suggestion that it may be derived from the O.E. haeg or O.N. hagi, an enclosure for pasture or hunting, seems less probable here. Aquas que dicitur Hee 1194.

**Kentmere:** The lake of the River Kent. 'Kent' is probably a British river-name derived from a word such as 'cunetio' meaning 'a sacred stream.' The O.E. 'mēre' was added later. The lake was drained for agricultural purposes late in the 19th century. Kenetemere 1240.

**Loweswater:** The leafy lake. This name seems to be related to a similar name given to a lake in Sweden—Lövsjön—meaning 'the leafy lake'. The O.E. waeter was added at a later date to give meaning to a name which had become incomprehensible. O.N. lauf + O.N. saer. Laweswatre c.1188.

**Rydal Water:** The lake in the valley where rye is grown. O.E. ryge + O.N. dalr (O.E. dael) + O.E. waeter. This lake was formerly known as Routhmere, a name derived from O.N. rauthi + O.E. mēre (see River Rothay—page 23). Ridale 1180.

**Thirlmere:** The lake with a gap. The 'gap' may have been the narrow strip of water which was a feature of the 'waist' of Thirlmere before the level of the lake was raised by the construction of the Manchester Waterworks' reservoir towards the end of the 19th century. A wooden bridge used to span the lake at this point. O.E. thyrel + O.E. mēre. Thyrelmere 1573.

**Ullswater:** Ulfr's lake. Ulfr was a common O.N. personal name. Ulveswatre 1323.

**Wastwater:** The name of the lake and the name of the valley have been merged: 'Wasdale' means 'the valley with the lake'; the lake itself was therefore superfluously described as a 'water'. Wassewatre 1294.

**Windermere:** Vinandr's lake. 'Vinandar' is the genitive form of the O.N. personal name 'Vinandr'. O.N. Vinandr + O.E. mēre. Wynandremer c.1180.

# The Tarns

**Angle Tarn:** The tarn shaped like a fish-hook (or, less directly, the fishing tarn). O.N. ongull + O.N. tjorn. Angilterne 1266.

**Blea Tarn:** The dark tarn or the deep-blue tarn. O.N. blá + O.N. tjorn. The name 'Blaatjernet', with the same meaning, is found in Norway. Bleaterne 1587.

**Blelham Tarn:** The dark pool or the deep-blue pool. O.N. blá + O.E. lumme * (the word 'Tarn' is superfluous here). Blalam 1539

**Blind Tarn:** The tarn with no outlet or the tarn overgrown with weed. O.E. or O.N. blind + O.N. tjorn. Blind Torn 1822.

**Boo Tarn:** This unusual name may be an abbreviation of the local name Booth or it may be derived from the O.N. personal name Bui or alternatively from the O.N. búth, a hut. The meaning could be therefore, either Booth's Tarn or Bui's Tarn or the tarn by the hut.

**Burnmoor Tarn:** No reliable derivation can be given for this name. One suggestion is that it may bear some relation to the numerous 'borrans' or burial cairns on the moor, but early forms of the name indicate insufficient evidence to suggest a trustworthy development of the modern name from the O.E. burgaesn which this would imply. Burman Tarne 1570.

**Dock Tarn:** The tarn of the water-lilies. O.E. docce + O.N. tjorn. Docketerne 1210.

**Floutern Tarn:** The 1343 form 'Flutern' does not offer specific help with this name, but it is possible that it may be derived from an O.N. word 'flói'* meaning 'a watery moss' which would not be inappropriate. The Icelandic 'flói' and the Lakeland dialect 'flow' have the same meaning. The second element is O.N. tjorn so the additional 'Tarn' is superfluous. 'The tarn in the watery moss.'

**Harrop Tarn:** The second element of this name is derived from O.E. hōp, an overhanging valley; the first element is more obscure but the most probable derivation may be from O.E. haer, a pile of rocks or stones. This would give 'the tarn in an overhanging valley littered with rocks and stones', an appropriate description for this particular spot Harhop 1280.

**Innominate Tarn:** This is a modern name replacing the earlier name 'LOAF TARN' which is said to refer to the clumps of peat in the tarn resembling pieces of risen dough.

**Kemp Tarn:** The warrior's tarn. O.E. cempe or O.N. kampi + O.N. tjorn. The modern personal name Kemp(e) is probably derived from the same source or from the O.N. personal name Kampi, itself acquired, doubtless, as the result of some prowess in battle.

**Knipe Tarn:** The tarn by the steep rock. O.N. gnípa + O.N. tjorn. Knype is found as a modern surname. Gnipe 1329.

**Lanty's Tarn:** 'Lanty' is a diminutive of the name 'Launcelot'. The original Launcelot is lost to history. It is unlikely to have been the legendary Lanty Slee, the 19th century moonshiner from Little Langdale.

**Levers Water:** Lafhere's tarn or the rushy tarn. Lafhere was an O.E. personal name. O.E. laefer + O.E. waeter.

**Lindeth Tarn:** The tarn under the hill with the lime trees. O.N. lind + O.N. hofuth (or O.E. lind + O.E. hēafod) + O.N. tjorn. Lindheued 1262.

**Low Birker Tarn:** The tarn by the shieling with the birch trees. O.N. bjork (plural birki) + O.N. erg + O.N. tjorn.

**Over Water:** Orri's tarn or the tarn where blackcock are found. Orri was an O.N. personal name probably derived from the same O.N. word which also meant a blackcock. Orre Water 1687.

**Potter Tarn:** The shieling by the deep pool. O.N. pot + O.N. erg + O.N. tjorn. 'Pot' is now a dialect word meaning a deep pool ('Tarn' is thus superfluous). Potergha 1245.

**Scales Tarn:** The tarn by the shepherd's hut. O.N. skáli + O.N. tjorn. Scales Tarn 1794.

**Siney Tarn:** The tarn which dries up. The dialect word 'sine' means to run dry. It is also found in the name Sinen Gill, a small beck which often runs dry. Sining Tarne 1587.

**Skeggles Water:** Skakull's tarn. Skakul is an O.N. personal name. Skakelswatre 1375.

**Sprinkling Tarn:** This is a modern name replacing 'Sparkling Tarn', a name used in 1774. Before this the tarn was known as 'Prentibiountern' (1322), a name which gave birth to the legend that the tarn was once associated with a miscreant Norseman, Björn, who was branded (prenti) for his crime—Prentibjörn's Tarn. Modern linguistic studies, however, indicate that it is not possible to reconcile the recorded name—Prentibioun—with these Old Norse words, and so an interesting and widely believed story must be thrown overboard. It is more probable that Prentibioun is derived from 'Sprentaburn', an O.E. compound word meaning 'the gushing or sparkling stream'. O.N. tjorn is added.

**Stickle Tarn:** The tarn by the prominent peak (in this case Harrison Stickle). O.E. sticele/O.N. stikill + O.N. tjorn.

**Styhead Tarn:** The tarn at the top of the path. O.N. stígr/O.E.

stig + O.N. hofuth/O.E. hēafod + O.N. tjorn (see STYHEAD PASS—page 52).

**Tewet Tarn:**   The peewit's tarn. 'Tewit' is a northern word for the peewit or lapwing. M.E. tuwytte + O.N. tjorn.

**Wiseen Tarn:**   The tarn among the willow trees. The dialect word 'withen' (willow trees) is derived from the O.E. withig from which we obtain the word 'withy', the branch of a willow or osier used for basket-making and for binding bundles.

**Blea Tarn—the dark or the deep-blue tarn**

# Rivers and Streams

**Aira Beck:** The stream with the gravel banks. O.N. eyrr + O.N. á + O.N. bekkr. Several similar names may be found in the Lune Valley (Ayre, Green Ayre, etc.), and in Iceland the stream-name 'Eyrara' has the same meaning. Ayrauhe beke c.1250.

**River Bleng:** The dark river. O.N. blæingr derived from O.N. blá. Bleng 1576.

**River Brathay:** The broad river. O.N. breithr + O.N. á. In former days this river was very prone to quick flooding and so was often of considerable breadth. It is also a fairly wide river in its lower reaches. Braitha c.1160.

**River Calder:** The rocky or rapid-flowing river. Welsh caled + Br. dubro* (Welsh dwfr). Caldre c.1200.

**River Caldew:** The cold river. O.E. cald + O.E. ēa. Caldeu 1189.

**River Cocker:** The crooked river. A British river-name probably derived from Br. kukrā* or crumbāco*, crooked. Koker 1170.

**River Crake:** The rocky river. A British river-name derived from Br. creic*, a rock. Craic 1196.

**Dacre Beck:** The trickling stream. A British river-name derived from Br. dakru* or Welsh deigr, a teardrop. Dacore c.730.

**River Derwent:** The river abounding in oak trees. A British river-name derived from Br. derw*, oak tree, and derwentio*, abounding in oak trees. The same British root is found in the River Dart in Devon, the River Darent in Kent, the River Darwen in Lancashire and the Yorkshire and Derbyshire Derwents.

**River Duddon:** No entirely reliable explanation of this name can be given. The forms found in the 12th century, Duthen and Duden, may indicate a derivation from an English personal name—Dudda—and from O.E. denu, a valley. In this case 'Duddon' would mean 'Dudda's valley'. An alternative suggestion is that the name is based on a lost British river-name containing the Welsh word 'du' meaning 'black' or 'dark'. 'The dark river' is a not uncommon description of Lakeland waters, but, at present, the etymology must remain rather doubtful.

**Dungeon Gill:** The name may come from association with the French or M.E. word 'donjon' implying a dark, subterranean place or even a cavern. In her **Journals**, Dorothy Wordsworth

21

refers to 'those fissures or caverns which in the language of the country are called dungeons'. The true meaning of the O.N. gil is a narrow ravine.

**River Eamont:** The meeting place of the rivers. O.E. ēa + O.E. (ge) mot. The junction of the Rivers Lowther and Eamont was once a meeting place of some importance as may be inferred from the nearby ancient monuments of Mayburgh, King Arthur's Table, the Roman fort of Brocavum and, if we are to believe the old legend, it was here that King Athelstan of Wessex, King Constantine of Scotland and King Owain of Cumbria met in 926 to resolve their differences. Eamotum 926.

**River Ehen:** This is probably a British river-name related to the Welsh 'iain' = cold. 'The cold river'.

**River Esk:** This is probably the British river-name 'Isca', similar to the River Exe in Devon and derived from the same root as the Welsh 'esk', water.

**Gasgale Gill:** The stream or ravine where the goat huts are found. O.N. geit + O.N. skáli + O.N. gil.

**River Gilpin:** This is an obscure name for which no really satisfactory linguistic origin has yet been offered. A probable derivation could be from an O.E. word such as 'gylping' meaning 'a gushing stream'. Gylpyne c.1600. The family name Gilpin appears frequently in the area from the 13th century.

**Goldrill Beck:** The brook where marigolds grow (marigold here refers to the kingcup). O.E. golde + O.E. rille (the O.N. bekkr is superfluous).

**Grains Gill:** The shieling which stands where the valleys fork. The 'fork' is near Stockley Bridge where Grains Gill and Styhead Gill meet. O.N. grein + O.N. skáli.

**Greenup Gill:** The stream in the green valley. O.E. grēne + O.E. hōp + O.N. gil. Grenehope c.1211.

**River Greta:** The rocky river. A Norwegian river, the Gryte, has the same meaning. O.N. grjót + O.N. á.

**River Irt:** No entirely satisfactory explanation of this name has yet been put forward as some doubt still surrounds Ekwall's suggestion that it may be derived from the Welsh 'ir' meaning 'fresh' or 'green'.

**River Kent:** This is probably a British river-name based on the word 'cunētio'* or 'cunētju'* indicating that the Kent was a sacred river. Kenet 1246.

**Launchy Gill:** Launchy is a diminutive of the name Launceld or Lawrence. O.N. gil.

**River Leven:** The smoothly-flowing river. This is probably a British river-name derived from a root similar to the Welsh 'llyfyn', smooth. Leuena c.1160.

**River Lickle:** An obscure name. Suggested derivations are from either O.N. lykkja, a curve or loop + O.N. hylr, a slow pool, or

Br. liwcyl*, bright or shining. These would give, respectively, 'the slow, curving stream' and 'the bright stream'. Licul 1140.

**River Liza:** The shining river. O.N. ljós + O.N. á. Lesar 1292.

**River Lowther:** The foaming river. O.N. lauthr + O.N. á. Lauther 1157.

**River Mint:** The noisy river. A British river-name from Br. mimeto*, noise. Mimet 1205.

**River Mite:** An obscure name probably of British origin and based on a root such as 'meigh',* meaning 'to urinate' or 'to drizzle' and so related to O.E. migan, O.N. miga and Latin mingere. The inspiration for such a name is open to speculation.

**Naddle Beck:** The stream in the wedge-shaped valley. O.N. naddr + O.N. dalr + O.N. bekkr. Naddale 1303.

**River Rothay:** The trout river. O.N. rauthi + O.N. á. O.N. rauthi literally means 'the red one' and it is possible that this was applied to the river-trout, a linguistic probability given colour by the well-established tradition that all the char from Lake Windermere go up to the River Brathay while all the trout go up the Rothay. Routha 1275.

**Smithy Beck:** The stream by the forge. An ancient smelting hearth is nearby.

**Sourmilk Gill:** Several Lakeland becks bear this name and it seems likely that it is a direct description of the white foam which is characteristic of these rapid and rocky mountain streams. The Sourmilk Gill in Easedale is referred to by Dorothy Wordsworth as Churnmilk Force.

**River Sprint:** The gushing river. O.N. spretta. Spret c.1195. (The 'n' was probably added by association with the nearby rivers Kent and Mint.)

**Stockghyll:** O.N. stokkr literally means 'a tree stump' and O.N. gil literally means 'a narrow ravine', but our word 'stock', derived from 'stokkr', is also used of a mill and we know that from the early Middle Ages a fulling mill existed in this valley. It is possible for Stockghyll to mean either 'a wooded ravine' or 'the ravine with the fulling mill'. (The spelling 'Ghyll' dates from the late 18th century and is incorrect. 'Gill' derives directly from O.N. 'gil'.)

**Taylorgill Force:** The waterfall in Taylor's ravine. The family of William Taylor is referred to in the Crosthwaite Parish Register for 1718 and it seems probable that the stream and the waterfall were named after him. O.N. gil + O.N. fors.

**Wren Gill:** This name did not originally refer to a gill but to a dale. In 1577 it was known as **WRANGDAYL** meaning 'the twisting valley'. O.N. vrangr + O.N. dalr. The 'dale' was replaced by 'gill' sometime during the 18th century.

# The Fells

**Allen Crags:**  Allen is a personal name common in England soon after the Norman Conquest. It is of Breton origin and its early form was Alein. The particular 'Alein' after whom this crag took its name is unknown.

**Arnison Crag:**  Arni was a Norse personal name and so 'Arnison' would be 'Arni's son' who gave his name to the crag. A possible alternative derivation might be from the O.E. earn + O.E. stān meaning 'the eagle's rock'.

**Barf:**  This was formerly known as Barrugh Fell (1821), indicating a derivation from O.N. berg, a mountain. Barugh is a northern surname and is correctly pronounced Barf.

**Basebrown:**  This is an example of an Inversion Compound (see page 13) and is probably derived from the O.N. personal name Bruni and O.N. báss—'Bruni's cowshed'. The surname Basbroun appears in the 16th century Cumberland Subsidy Rolls. Basebrun 1216.

**Beda Head:**  No reliable explanation can be given of this name. It is possible that 'Bed ...' may be the remnants of a personal name (Bede?) and the ending 'a' may be, here as elsewhere, the common abbrevation of 'how' (O.N. haugr). This would suggest 'Bede's hill' as a probable meaning for this fell.

**Birkett Fell:**  Named in honour of Lord Birkett who in 1962 played a decisive part in preventing, temporarily at least, the exploitation of Ullswater by the Manchester Water Authority.

**Black Combe:**  The dark crested mountain. O.E. blaec + O.E. camb. One of the features of Black Combe is the dark heather which grows there.

**Blencathra:**  The first element here is the Welsh word 'blaen', a summit. The second element is more difficult, but a likely explanation is that it comes from the Welsh 'cateir', a chair, as in Cader Idris. This would be an apt descripton of the summit's shape as seen from many angles. The name 'Saddleback' by which this fell is often known does not appear until 1769. Blenkarthure 1589.

**Bowfell:**  The usual explanation of this name—the bow-shaped fell —is not consistent with the early (1242) form which was 'Bowesfel', clearly indicating the use of a personal name. The

24

surname Bowe appears in a Cumberland deed of 1333. It is also significant that the pass below Bowfell, now known as Three Tarns, was formerly called 'Bowesscard' or 'Bowe's scarth'— O.N. skarth.

**Brandreth:** The O.N. words 'brand-reith', a fire-place or grate, came to mean more specifically a grid-iron or trivet. A reference of 1805 which refers to this fell as 'the three-footed Brandreth' seems to be consistent with this derivation and suggests that a beacon once burned on the summit.

**Buckbarrow:** The hill of the buck or goat. The name may be derived from either O.E. bucc (O.N. bokkr), a buck, or from O.E. bucca (O.N. bokki), a he-goat. The second element is O.E. beorg (O.N. berg), a hill. Bokkebèrge c.1400.

**Calva:** The hill where calves are pastured. O.E. calf (O.N. kálfr) + O.N. haugr.

**Carling Knott:** The hill where the old woman lives. O.N. kerling + O.N. knútr.

**Carrock Fell:** The rocky fell. Old Welsh carrec + O.N. fjall.

**Cat Bells:** The den of the wild cat. The wild cat was common in the area until the early 19th century. O.E. catt + M.E. belde.

**Catstycam:** The crest or ridge with a steep, wild-cat's path. O.E. camb (O.N. kambr) + O.E. stig (O.N. stígr) + O.E. catt (O.N. kattr).

**Causey Pike:** The peak above the causeway. The reference is probably to the Roman road which ran across the low-lying land between Crosthwaite and Braithwaite and which appears in 1280 as 'le chaucey', the causeway. O.E. pīc (O.N. pík).

**Caw Fell:** The hill where calves are pastured. O.E. calf (O.N. kalfr) + O.N. fjall.

**Cofa Pike:** Cofa is variant of Calva and Caw Fell; it also lies at the head of Caw Cove. Its origin is almost certainly the same: the hill where calves are pastured. The 'a' of Cofa is an abbreviated form of 'how', a hill. O.E. calf (O.N. kalfr) + O.N. haugr + O.E. pīc (O.N. pík).

**Crinkle Crags:** This name is generally supposed to be a reference to the serrated or wrinkled appearance of the crags which form the summit line of the fell. O.E. cringol = wrinkled, twisted.

**Dodd** (Great, Little): A rounded hill, usually grassy or bare. M.E. dodde—which survives in Lakeland dialect and has the same meaning.

**Dollywagon Pike:** The origin of this unusual name is not known, but it seems improbable that it is derived from an early name bearing any resemblance to it.

**Dove Crag:** The crag frequented by doves or pigeons. This is probably a modern name.

**Dow Crag:** The early forms of this name, 'Dove Crag' and 'Doe Crag', suggest that at one time the fell was frequented by doves or deer or both.

**Dunmallet:** This prominent hill overlooking Ullswater was certainly an ancient British fort—the gaelic 'dun' indicates a hill-fort —but its precise origin is less certain. The name may have come from a British chieftain, Mallok, and so mean 'Mallok's fort'. It may also be derived from the Gaelic word 'mallacht' meaning 'curses'. Early forms, 'Dunmalloght' and 'Dunmallock', could justify either interpretation. 'Mallock's fort' or 'the cursed fort'. Dunmallok 1329.

**Eel Crag:** The steep or precipitous crag. O.N. illr.

**Esk Pike:** Formerly known as 'Tongue Fell' (O.N. tunga) this fell was renamed after the River Esk by the Reverend Clifton Ward in modern times. The 'tongue' referred to in the original name lies between Angle Tarn and Allen Crags Gill.

**Fairfield:** This fell was formerly, and more precisely, known as Rydal Head. Its present name is self-explanatory—'the fair or pleasant fell'. (Field = fell).

**Fleetwith Pike:** No early forms of this name are known, but it may be associated with the northern dialect word 'fleet' used to indicate 'a flat area or bog in the hills from which water flows'. The high plateau on Fleetwith is the source of both Gatescarth Beck and Warnscale Beck. The remaining elements in the name are probably the O.N. vithr, a wood, and O.E. pīc (O.N. pík). A possible meaning could, therefore, be 'the peak on the wooded fleet'.

**Froswick:** The normal meaning of 'wick' (O.E. wic) is 'a dairy farm'. This would seem rather inappropriate here and the name at present remains obscure. The first element may be the remnant of a personal name such as Frosti.

**Gimmer Crag:** 'Gimmer' is the Cumbrian term for a yearling sheep (O.N. gymbr), and there may have been some local history concerning this particular crag and a crag-fast sheep.

**Glaramara:** The 1210 version of this name was 'Hovedgleuer-merhe', a compound word which can be analysed as follows: 'hoved = O.N. hofuth, signifying the mass of the fell; 'gleurm' = the dative plural 'gliufrum' of O.N. gliúfr, meaning 'by the ravines; 'erhe' = O.N. erg, a shieling or mountain hut. The whole name, therefore, means 'the mountain with the shieling by the ravines'.

**Gowbarrow:** The windy hill. O.N. gol + O.N. berg. Golbery c.1150.

**Grasmoor:** The grassy upland. O.E. grass + O.E. mōr.

**Great Cockup:** The valley where the woodcock are found. 'Cock' in place-names usually refers to the woodcock; 'up' = O.E. hōp.

**Great Gable:** The 14th century form, Mykelgavel, is derived from O.N. mikill, great, and O.N. gafl, gable. The description almost certainly refers to the shape of the fell which from several viewpoints resembles the gable of a house.

**Green Gable:** The 'green' is in contrast to the bare rock of the

**Pike o' Stickle—the peak with the sharp summit**

crags of Great Gable towering over this smaller neighbour. 'Gable' is O.N. gafl as in Great Gable.

**Grike:** 'Grike' is a Cumbrian dialect word for a cleft or narrow ravine such as may be found on the north face of this fell. This must be the origin of the name.

**Grisedale Pike:** The peak above the valley of the pigs. O.N. griss + O.N. dalr + O.E. pīc (O.N. pík).

**Hallin Fell:** This may be derived from O.N. hallr, a slope, with the O.N. definite article -inn as the second element. The meaning would then be simply 'the hillslope' but early forms are unhelpful here. The 'Fell' is superfluous. Halin 1277.

**Hardknott:** The rough, craggy fell. O.N. harthr + O.N. knútr. Hardecnut c.1210.

**Harrison Stickle:** This is almost certainly an O.N. personal name which by the Middle Ages had become a local family name. The original name is uncertain. The final element is O.E. sticele O.N. stikill = a steep place.

**Harter Fell:** The hart's fell. O.N. hjartar = of the hart (genitive of O.N. hjortr) + O.N. fjall. Herterfel 1210.

**Haycock:** This may be a descriptive name suggested by the idea of similarity between the shape of the fell and that of a large haycock. A linguistic explanation may be more likely since the term 'haycock' meaning a heap of hay was not used until the late Middle Ages: O.N. hár + O.N. kökkr = 'a high lump or heap'.

**Haystacks:** As with Haycock this name is also often regarded as purely descriptive and in his *Guide to the Lakes* (1778), Thomas West commented that it 'is by the dalesmen from its form called Hayrick'. It is probably more accurate to explain the name in linguistic terms and it would appear to be derived from O.N. hár + O.N. stakkr = 'high rocks', an equally descriptive origin.

**Helm Crag:** The O.N. word 'hjálmr' may mean either 'a helmet' or 'a cattleshed'. The fell does bear resemblance to a helmet from certain viewpoints and this seems more likely to have been the original inspiration. So—'the crag which looks like a helmet'.

**Helvellyn:** This—perhaps the best known of all the Lakeland fells—has not yet yielded up the secret of its name. Many suggestions have been made, but none is so far acceptable to the linguistic experts. No very early forms exist.

**Heron Pike:** This may be derived from O.E. earn, an eagle, or from M.E. heroun, a heron. The former seems more likely. O.E. earn (O.N. ornr) + O.E. pīc (O.N. pík): 'the eagle's peak'.

**High Spy:** An obscure name. It may mean simply 'a look-out post', referring to some lost fort.

**High Street:** This is a modern name referring to the Roman road which runs over the fell close to the line of the summit ridge. There was a highroad here long before the Romans came known as Bretesstrete, the Britons' road.

**Hindscarth:** The pass used by the red deer. O.N. hind + O.N. skarth.

**Hobcarton:** The first element here seems to be O.N. hóp, an enclosed valley (although it has been unconvincingly suggested that it might be from O.E. hobbe, a mound or tussock). The second element is probably an O.N. personal name, Kjártan, after whom the valley was named. Hopecartan 1260. An inversion compound (see page 13).

**Hopegill Head:** The headland by the narrow ravine (at the end of the valley). O.E. hōp + O.N. gil + O.E. hēafod.

**Ill Bell:** The bell-shaped hill. O.E. hyll + O.N. bjalli.

**Illgill Head:** The headland on the hill with a narrow ravine. O.E. hyll + O.N. gil + O.E. hēafod. It is also possible that the first element may be derived from O.N. illr meaning steep or precipitous, which as one looks down to Wastwater seems a very apt description.

**Kidsty Pike:** The peak by the steep path for young goats. M.E. kide (O.N. kith) + O.N. stígr + O.E. pīc (O.N. pík).

**Kirk Fell:** The fell above the church. O.N. kirkja + O.N. fjall. The tiny church at Wasdale Head stands in the fields at the foot of Kirk Fell.

**Latrigg:** Early forms of this name do not include the element 'rigg' (O.N. hryggr) which usually indicates a ridge with steep falls on each side. This scarcely applies to Latrigg and its early name Laterhayheved (c.1210) has no such descriptive term. This form may be analysed into O.N. látr + O.E. haeg + O.E. hēafod. 'The hill where animals had a lair and where there was a hunting enclosure.'

**Latterbarrow:** The hill where animals had their lair. O.N. látr + O.N. berg. A Norwegian dialect word, letre, meaning a shelter for farm animals, and cognate with O.N. látr, may indicate a more precise explanation of this name.

**Ling Mell:** The heather-covered hill. O.N. lyng + Welsh moel.

**Loadpot Hill:** The hill with the deep hole where ore was worked. O.E. lād = a vein of ore (a load) + M.E. potte. A vein of haematite was found near the summit and was worked for some years. Remains of these workings may still be seen there.

**Loughrigg:** The ridge above the lake. Gael. loch + O.N. hryggr. Loghrigg 1274.

**Maiden Moor:** The name 'Maiden' is given to many prehistoric hillforts, but no satisfactory reason for this has yet been forthcoming. It may refer to a fortress which has never been taken (e.g. Péronne in France was known as La Pucelle, the Virgin) but there is no evidence so far to suggest that a fort may have existed on Maiden Moor. It may be a name corrupted beyond analysis or we may speculate that the moor may have been associated with some long-lost tradition concerning maidens. E.P.N.S. makes the interesting suggestion that the many 'Maiden' place-names might indicate sites associated with games or rituals in which maidens took part, drawing a parallel with the place-name 'Julian Bower', which is found in Cumbria and in three other English counties, with its echoes of the Julian Games referred to in Virgil's Aeneid. The Swedish place-name Tröjemala has quite specific associations with such games but no evidence is so far forthcoming for the English sites.

**Mellbreak:** An obscure name. A possible derivation might be from Welsh moel, a bare hill + O.N. brekka, a hillslope (often referring to a hill which falls to a water's edge as Mellbreak does). Mellbreack 1778.

**Mell Fell:** This is the Welsh 'moel', a bare hill, with O.N. fjall added at a later date.

**Nab Scar:** The projecting ridge with a steep crag. O.N. nabbi + O.N. sker.

**Old Man of Coniston:** 'Man' is a northern dialect word meaning a large cairn such as that which marks the summit of this fell.

**Orrest Head:** The hill where a battle took place. O.N. orrusta + O.N. hofuth/O.E. hēafod. The nature and date of such a battle are unknown.

**Pavey Ark:** A deed of the 13th century refers to 'Pavia filia Willelmi', Pavia the daughter of William. This suggests that 'Pavey' may be derived from this feminine name. 'Ark' is probably a corruption of O.N. erg, a shieling. 'Pavia's shieling.'

**Pike o' Blisco:** This name is unexplained.

**Pike o' Stickle:** The peak with the sharp summit. O.E. pīc (O.N. pík) + O.N. stikill.

**Pillar:** This is a modern name given to the mountain by virtue of its association with the famous rock. Its earlier name is uncertain.

**Place Fell:** The 1266 version of this name—Plescefel—suggests that it may have originated with the O.E. plæsce, an open, marshy place. The wide plateau of the summit area of Place Fell may once have been such a spot: + O.N. fjall.

**Rainsborrow Crag:** An obscure name. It may be derived from O.N. hrafn + O.N. berg with M.E. cragge added later; this would give the not inappropriate meaning 'the crag on the hill where ravens live.'

**Rampsgill Head:** Two meanings are possible here. (a) the hill with the ravine where wild garlic grows. O.N. hramsa + O.N. gil + O.N. hofuth/O.E. hēafod; (b) the hill with the ravine where ravens live. O.N. hrafn + O.N. gil + O.N. hofuth/O.E. hēafod. (Hrafn could also be a personal name.)

**Rest Dodd:** Obscure. A possible derivation might be from O.N. hrjóstr + M.E. dodde. 'The rough round hill.'

**Robinson:** A Richard Robinson purchased land in this area in the reign of Henry VIII and the fell is named after him.

**Rossett Pike:** This may be a contraction of Rosthwaite Pike meaning 'the peak above the clearing with the heap of stones': O.N. hreysi + O.N. thveit + O.E. pīc (O.N. pík). It might also be derived from O.N. hross + O.N. sætr, 'the peak by the high pastures where horses were kept'.

**Sail:** The swampy hill. O.N. seyla.

**St. Sunday Crag:** St. Dominic's crag. St. Dominic was often referred to as St. Sunday from the Latin 'dies Dominica', the Lord's Day. Why this crag should have acquired St. Dominic's name is not clear.

**Scafell. Scafell Pike:** The origin of these names is a little obscure, but the most likely explanations are those given by Ekwall and the English Place-name Society as follows: Ekwall: O.N. skáli + O.N. fjall = the fell with the shieling. E.P.N.S.: O.N. skalli + O.N. fjall = the fell with the bare summit. 'Skalli' might also be a nickname, 'Baldy'. Skallfield 1578.

**Scoat Fell:** The fell with the rocky projecting ridge. O.N. skúti or O.N. skót + O.N. fjall. Le Scote 1338.

**Seat Allen:** Alein's mountain shieling. An inversion compound (see page 13). Breton personal name, Alein + O.N. sætr.

**Seat Sandal:** Sandulfr's mountain shieling. An inversion compound (see page 13). O.N. personal name, Sandulfr + O.N. sætr.

**Sergeant Man:** 'Man' is a dialect word for a large cairn. The sergeant may have been an official of Lord Egremont's estate and the tall cairn was probably a boundary mark, perhaps the county boundary at this point.

**Shap Fell:** The fell near the heap of stones. O.E. hēap + O.N. fjall. Hep. c.1175. The additional 's' in front of the 'h' of the early form 'Hep' is an unusual linguistic development which may also be found in the name Shoulthwaite (page 44). The heap of stones may have been the remains of the Stone Circle which stood nearby.

**Sheffield Pike:** This is probably a corruption of 'Sheep Fell' or "Sheep Fold" with O.E. pīc added. O.E. scēap + O.N. fjall or O.E. fald.

**Skiddaw:** There has been much speculation concerning the origin of this name. The second element is probably O.N. haugr, a hill, but the first element 'Skidd' is elusive. Early forms of the name— Skythou (1260), Skythowe (1343), and Skythow (1450)—all have a 'y' which has suggested a derivation from O.N. skyti, an archer. The same O.N. word is also a by-form of O.N. skúti, a craggy ridge, which may not seem entirely appropriate when applied to Skiddaw. Neither of these explanations accounts fully for the 'th' in all the early forms and an alternative suggestion is that the name is derived from O.N. skith (Icelandic—skitha) meaning 'firewood' or 'chopped billets of wood.' Three meanings, then, are suggested: 'the archer's hill'; 'the hill with a craggy ridge'; and 'the hill where firewood is found.'

**Slight Side:** The mountain shieling with the level pastures. O.N. sletta + O.N. sætr.

**Souther Fell:** The shoemaker's fell. O.N. sútari + O.N. fjall. Souterfell 1323.

**Starling Dodd:** This is an Inversion Compound (see page 13). The first element is O.N. stígr and the second is a Breton name Alein. 'Dodd' was added later. The meaning is, therefore, 'the bare, round hill by Alein's path', an explanation supported by medieval records which refer to a boundary path running from Blea Tarn 'to the path of Styalein'. Styalein 1230.

**Steel Fell:** The fell with a steep path. O.E. stigel + O.N. fjall.

**Swirl How:** Obscure. A Norwegian dialect word 'svirle', to swirl or whirl around, suggests that there may have been an O.N. word of similar meaning. This fell could appropriately be described as 'the hill where the wind swirls round'. How = O.N. haugr.

**Thunacar Knot:** Doubtful. O.N. knútr for the second feature seems clear, but 'thunacar' may be derived with less certainty from two O.N. words—'thunr', thin, and O.N. 'karr', a man. A probable explanation therefore could be 'the craggy hill of the thin man'.

**Ullock Pike:** The peak where the wolves play. O.N. úlfr + O.N. leikr + O.E. p̄īc (O.N. pík). Ulvelaik 1279.

**Ullscarf:** The wolf's pass. O.N. úlfr + O.N. skarth. Ulvescarth 1203.

**Wandhope:** The valley where osiers grow. O.N. vandr + O.N. hóp. The name of the valley was transferred to the fell.

**Wansfell:** Obscure. The first element may be a personal name. The nearest parallel may be in the famous earthwork, the Wansdyke, named after the Norse god, Woden. Could Wansfell be Woden's fell?

**Wether Hill. Wetherlam:** Both names appear to refer to the wether or castrated ram (from O.N. vethr).

**Whin Fell. Whinlatter. Whin Rigg:** The common element here is the O.N. word 'hvin'*, (M.E. whinne), furze or gorse, with O.N. fjall, Gaelic lettir, and O.N. hryggr added. 'The furze-covered fell, slope, ridge.'

**Whiteless Pike:** The origin of this name is unknown.

**Whiteside:** The white mountain shieling. O.N. hvitr + O.N. sætr.

**Yewbarrow:** The hill where ewes are pastured. O.E. ēowu + O.E. beorg. Yowberg 1322.

**Yoke:** The origin of this name is unknown. The Yoak 1778.

**Nan Bield Pass. The obvious explanation of Nan Bield is 'Ann's hut
or shelter'** (see page 51)

# The Valleys

**Allerdale:**  The valley of the River Ellen. The first element is derived from a British river-name with the O.N. genitive ending -ar added: of the Ellen. The O.N. dalr forms the final element as in all the dales. Alnerdale 1060.

**Bannerdale:**  The valley of the holly trees. The 13th century form of this name is the key to its origin and meaning: Baynewicdale = O.N. bein + O.N. vithr + O.N. dalr. The literal meaning of this is 'bone-wood dale', a reference to the white wood of the holly tree.

**Blengdale:**  The valley of the dark river. O.N. blæingr + O.N. dalr. Ekwall suggests that 'blæingr' is an O.N. river-name.

**Boardale:**  The valley with the herdsman's hut or storehouse. O.E. būr or O.N. búr + O.N. dalr or O.E. dael. Burdal 1250.

**Borrowdale:**  The valley of the fort. O.N. borgar (of the fort) + O.N. dalr. Borgordale 1170. Castle Crag in the Derwentwater Borrowdale is thought to have been a hill-fort of the Romano-British period; the eastern Borrowdale has a Roman fort. It is also possible, as some early forms seem to imply, that the O.N. word 'á', a river, may be part of this name. If so this would give borgar + á + dalr, the valley of the fort by the river.

**Bowderdale:**  The valley with the herdsman's hut. O.N. búthar + O.N. dalr. Boutherdal 1322.

**Caudale:**  The valley of the calves. O.E. calf (O.N. kalfr) + O.N. dalr (O.E. dæl). Cawdell 1187.

**Coledale:**  The valley of the charcoal burners. O.N. kola + O.N. dalr. It is possible that the first element might be a Norse personal name, perhaps Kolli, in which case the meaning would be 'Kolli's valley'.

**Croasdale:**  The valley with the cross. O.N. kross + O.N. dalr. A 'cross' was usually a wayside cross perhaps indicating a preaching spot from the days of the Celtic mission.

**Deepdale:**  The deep valley. O.N. djúp + O.N. dalr. Diupdal 1184.

**Dovedale:**  The valley of the doves. O.N. dúfa + O.N. dalr. It is possible that this may be a modern name in which case the O.N. analysis is speculative.

**Dunnerdale:**  The valley of the River Duddon. O.N. duthnar (genitive—of Dudda) + O.N. dalr. Dunerdal 1293. See under 'Rivers' for 'Duddon' (page 21).

**Easedale:** Asi's valley. O.N. personal name, Asi + O.N. dalr. Asedale 1293.

**Ennerdale:** The valley of the River Ehen. 'Ehen is probably a British river-name related to the Welsh 'iain' meaning 'cold': + O.N. dalr. Eghnerdale 1321. Before the 14th century the valley was known as Anenderdale (1135) or Anand's valley from an O.N. personal name.

**Eskdale:** The valley of the River Esk. 'Esk' is probably a British river-name, Isca*, related to the Welsh 'esk' = water: + O.N. dalr.

**Fusedale:** The valley with a cattle byre. O.N. fé-hús + O.N. dalr. Fehusdale 1278.

**Grisedale. Grizedale:** Both names are identical and have the same derivation: 'the valley of the pigs'. O.N. griss + O.N. dalr.

**Kentdale:** The valley of the River Kent. 'Kent' is thought to be an old British river-name indicating 'a sacred river' (see under River Kent—page 22) + O.N. dalr.

**Keskadale:** The valley with Ketil's shieling. O.N. personal name, Ketil (common locally until the early Middle Ages) + O.N. skáli + O.N. dalr. Ketelschaledal 1268.

**Langdale:** The long valley. The original name was Langedene (1157) derived from O.E. lang + O.E. denu, a long wooded valley. The word 'dene' is uncommon in Lakeland and was later replaced by the more usual O.N. dalr, a dale, O.N. langr + O.N. dalr.

**Long Sleddale:** The long valley. The O.E. word 'slæd', a valley, forms the first element of Sleddale, and the O.N. dalr was added later, thus duplicating the word. The word 'long' does not appear in early forms of the name. O.N. langr + O.E. slæd + O.N. dalr. Sledale c.1200.

**Mardale:** The valley with a lake. O.E. mere + O.N. dalr (O.E. dæl). The 'mere' referred to is the original and smaller Haweswater. Merdale 1278.

**Martindale:** St. Martin's valley. Local legend asserts that the valley received its name from St. Martin, Bishop of Tours, renowned for his missionary work in remote rural areas in France, and greatly admired by St. Ninian, the Celtic missionary in north-west Britain. A cross dedicated to St. Martin stood in the valley before 1266. Martinedale 1184.

**Matterdale:** The valley where the madder plant grows. O.N. mathra + O.N. dalr. Matherdale 1323. The root of the madder plant (Rubia tinctorum) was a source of natural dye for the early textile industry.

**Miterdale:** The valley of the River Mite. 'Mite' is thought to be of British origin and related to a root such as 'meigh'*, to urinate or drizzle. See under River Mite—page 23.

**Mosedale:** The valley of the peat mosses or peat bogs. O.N. mosi +

35

O.N. dalr. There are four Mosedales and six Mosedale Becks in the Lake District.

**Mungrisedale:** The valley of the pigs with a church dedicated to St. Mungo. The original name was O.N. griss + dalr, and St. Mungo's name was added at a later date with the building of the valley church. St. Mungo, also known as St. Kentigern, was a 6th century missionary in north-west Britain. Mounge Grieesdell 1600.

**Newlands:** The new lands. The lower area of Newlands first came under cultivation following the draining of Uzzicar Tarn in the 14th century. Neulandes 1318.

**Patterdale:** Patrick's valley. Tradition holds that St. Patrick worked as a missionary here, baptising at the local well. It seems more likely that the Patrick who did give his name to this valley was a Norse-Irish settler of a much later date. Patrichesdale 1184.

**Rannerdale:** The valley of the ravens. O.N. hrafnar (genitive— of the ravens) + O.N. dalr.

**Riggindale:** The valley below the ridge. M.E. rigging + O.N. dalr. Regendale 1522.

**Rydale:** The valley where rye is grown. O.E. ryge (O.N. rugr) + O.N. dalr (O.E. dæl). Ridale 1180.

**Scandale:** The short valley. O.N. skammr + O.N. dalr. Skamdal 1277.

**Swindale:** The valley where the swine pasture. O.N. svin + O.N. dalr.

**Troutdale:** This name is little more than a century old. A trout hatchery was established here in the mid-19th century.

**Wasdale:** The valley with a lake. O.N. vatnsdalr. Wassedale 1279. The eastern Wasdale also had a lake, which was drained.

**Woundale:** There is no clear explanation of this name. A 'Woundale' in Shropshire is said to be derived from O.E. wunden wella, 'a twisting or winding stream'. This would also be appropriate here, especially as the 'valley' is not a 'dale' in the usual sense. Woundell 1560.

**The Stonethwaite Valley. Stonethwaite means 'the stony clearing'**
(see page 45)

# Towns, Villages, Hamlets and Farms

**Ambleside:** The pastures by the river sandbanks. O.N. á + O.N. melr + O.N. sætr. Amelsate 1274. The intrusive letter 'b' does not appear until the late 15th century and has no meaningful significance.

**Applethwaite:** The clearing where apple trees grow. O.E. æppel/ O.N. epli + O.N. thveit. Apelthwayt c.1220.

**Armathwaite:** The clearing where the hermit lives. O.E. ermite + O.N. thveit. Ermitethwayt 1292.

**Armboth:** Arni's hut. O.N. personal name, Arni + O.N. búth. Armabothe 1530.

**Ashness:** The headland where ash trees grow. O.N. eski (O.E. æsc) + O.N. nes. Eskness 1209. The O.E. æsc has a pronunciation much closer to the modern 'ash' than the O.N. eski.

**Askham:** Among the ash trees. O.N. ask(r) + -um (the dative plural). Askum 1275.

**Aughertree:** The old cottage in the secluded nook of land. O.E. ald + O.E. cot + O.N. vrá. Alcotewraye 1540.

**Barton:** The barley farm. O.E. bere + O.E. tūn. Bartun 1086. A barton later came to mean a grange or outlying farm.

**Beckermet:** The stream where the hermit lives. O.N. bekkr + O.E. ermite Becheremet c.1160.

**Bewaldeth:** Aldgyth's homestead. O.N. bú + O.E. feminine name, Aldgyth. An inversion compound—see page 13. Bualdith 1255.

**Birker:** The shieling by the birch trees. O.N. birki + O.N. erg. Birkergh 1272.

**Birkrigg:** The ridge with the birch trees. O.N. birki + O.N. hryggr. Birkeryg 1293.

**Blawith:** The dark wood. O.N. blá + O.N. vithr. Blawit 1276.

**Boot:** The bend in the valley. M.E. bouzht (O.E. boga). Bought 1587. The name refers to the angle in the valley at the junction of the River Esk and Whillan Beck. The 1587 version leaves open the possibility that the Northern dialect word 'bought', a sheepfold, might also be considered here.

**Bootle:** The dwelling house. O.E. bótl. Botle c.1135.

**Bowness:** The bull's headland. O.E. bula + O.N. nes. Bulnes 1282. Bowness on Solway has quite a different origin—from O.E. boga

+ næss /O.N. bogi + nes, the bow-shaped headland.

**Braithwaite:** The wideclearing. O.N. breithr + O.N. thveit. Braythwayt 1230.

**Brantwood:** The burnt wood. O.E. brende + O.E. wudu. Brentwood 1336.

**Brigsteer:** The bridge used by young bullocks (or steers). O.E. stēor + O.E. brycg. An alternative interpretation is based on the derivation from an O.N. personal name, Styrr, itself originating from O.N. stjórr, a young bullock or steer. In this case the first element would probably be O.N. brygga, a bridge, and the name would be an inversion compound (see page 13). Brygstere 1227. The bridge would probably have been a causeway across Underbarrow Pool to the pastures on Helsington Moor.

**Brotherilkeld** (also known as **Butterilket**): Ulfketil's huts. O.N. búthir (plural of O.N. búth) + O.N. personal name, Ulfketil, abbreviated to Ulfkil. An inversion compound (see page 13). The name Ulfketil was fairly common in the Lake District until the 14th century. Butherulkil 1242.

**Broughton-in-Furness:** The farmstead or hamlet by the stream. O.E. brōc + O.E. tūn. Brocton 1196. The 'in-Furness' was added to distinguish this place from several other Broughtons in the north-west.

**Butterwick:** The butter farm. O.E. butere + O.E. wíc. Buttyrwyk 1246. Cf. Keswick—the cheese farm.

**Caldbeck:** The cold stream. O.E. cald + O.N. bekkr. Caldbec 1212.

**Cartmel:** The sandbank by the rocky ground. O.N. kartr* + O.N. melr. Cartmel 1135. The village lies by the River Eea with a rocky ridge to the east.

**Castlerigg:** The fort on the ridge. O.E. castel (from Latin castellum) + O.N. hyrggr. Castelrigg. No trace of any fortification has so far been found at Castlerigg.

**Claife:** The steep hill. O.N. kleif. Clayf 1275.

**Clappersgate:** The path over the stepping stones or over a bridge made of stones (over the River Brathay). 'Clappers' are large flat stones or planks resting on stones to form a rough type of bridge; 'gate' is O.N. gata, a pathway. Clappergate 1588.

**Cockley Beck:** The stream where the woodcock play. 'Cock' in local place-names usually refers to the woodcock. The second element 'ley' is O.N. leikr, to play, and probably refers to the mating dance of these birds. Cocklayc 1189.

**Colwith:** The wood where charcoal is burned. O.E. col + O.N. vithr.

**Coniston:** The king's farm. O.E. cyning/O.N. konungr + O.E. tūn. Coningeston c.1160.

**Crook:** The bend or crook (in the river). O.N. krókr. Crok 1170.

**Crosthwaite:** The clearing with the cross. O.N. kross + O.N. thveit. Crostweit c.1150.

39

**Cunsey:** The king's river or the king's island. O.Dan. kunungs + O.N. á or O.N. ey.

**Dacre:** The trickling brook. A British river-name probably derived from Welsh 'deigr' or Br. 'dacru'*, a teardrop. The village is named after the stream. Dacor c.1125.

**Dalegarth:** The valley with the enclosed pasture or farmstead. O.N. dalr + O.N. garthr. Before the 16th century, Dalegarth was known as Austhwaite meaning 'Afaster's clearing' from O.N. personal name, Afaster + O.N. thveit.

**Dockray:** The corner of land overgrown with docks or sorrel. O.E. docce + O.N. vrá. Docwra 1278.

**Dowthwaitehead:** Dufa's clearing. O.N. feminine name, Dufa + O.N. thveit. Dowethweyt 1285.

**Drigg:** The place of portage: i.e. the place where boats had to be carried or dragged over an unnavigable stretch of water—here the River Irt. O.N. drag or dreg. Dreg c.1180.

**Egremont:** A Norman-French name recorded early in the 12th century shortly after the norman settlement in Cumbria. It seems likely that the castle was named after Aigremont in Normandy with possibly a reference to the prominent knoll on which it was built.

**Ellers:** The field overgrown with alder bushes. O.N. elri. Ellersfielde 1578.

**Embleton:** Eanbald's farmstead. O.E. personal name, Eanbald + O.E. tūn. Emelton 1195.

**Finsthwaite:** Finn's clearing. O.N. personal name, Finn + O.N. thveit. Fynnesthwayt 1336.

**Foulsyke:** The muddy stream or ditch. O.E. fūl/O.N. fúll + O.E. sīc/O.N. sík. Fullsyke 1587.

**Gamblesby:** Gamel's farmstead. O.N. personal name Gamall + O.N. býr. Gamelesbi 1177.

**Gatesgarth:** The pass where the goats go. O.N. geit + O.N. skarth. Gaitescarth 1318.

**Gillerthwaite:** The clearing where snares are set. O.N. gildri + O.N. thveit. Gillerthwait 1604.

**Glencoyne:** The reedy glen. Welsh glyn + Welsh cawn. Glencoine 1589.

**Glenridding:** The glen overgrown with bracken. Welsh glyn + Welsh rhedyn. Glenredyn 1292.

**Gosforth:** The goose ford. O.E. gōs + O.E. ford. Goseford c. 1150. The change from 'ford' to 'forth' is fairly common in the northern counties.

**Grange-in-Borrowdale:** A grange was an outlying farm or granary. This 'grange' was part of the Borrowdale property of Furness Abbey. M.E./O.Fr. grange. Grangia nostra de Boroudale 1396.

**Grassguards:** The grassy enclosure. O.N. gres + O.N. garthr. Gresgards 1599.

**Green Quarters:** The grassy quarter. This was one of the four sub-divisions—quarters—of the township of Kentmere. The other three were Crag, Hollowbank and Wray. (1760). O.E. grēne —green in the sense of grassy.

**Gutherscale:** Godric's hut. O.N. personal name, Godric + O.N. skáli. Goderikeschales 1318.

**Hartsop:** The valley of the hart. O.E. heorot + O.E. hōp. Herteshope c. 1184.

**Haverigg:** The hill where oats are grown. O.N. hafri + O.N. hryggr. Haverig c.1180.

**Haverthwaite:** The clearing where oats are grown. O.N. hafri + O.N. thveit. Haverthwayt 1336.

**Hawkshead:** Haukr's shieling. O.N. personal name, Haukr + O.N. sætr. Houksete c.1200.

**Hesket Newmarket:** The hillside where ash trees grow. O.N. eski + O.E. hēafod. Eskhevid c.1230. The word 'Newmarket' was added at a later date, but it is not known when a market was established here.

**Hollens/Hollins:** The place where the holly bushes grow. O.E. holegn.

**Holmrook:** The 'island' in the bend of the river. O.N. holmr + O.N. krókr. Holmcrooke 1569.

**Howtown:** The farmstead on the hill. O.N. haugr + O.E. tūn.

**Hutton Roof:** Rolf's farmstead on the ridge. O.E. hōh + O.E. tūn + O.N. personal name, Hróthúlfr (Rolf). Hoton Roff 1316. An inversion compound (see page 13).

**Ickenthwaite:** The clearing where squirrels are found. O.N. ikorni + O.N. thveit. Yccornethwaite c.1535.

**Ings:** The meadows or outlying pastures. O.N. eng. The Inges 1546.

**Ireby:** The Irishman's farm. O.N. Iri + O.N. býr. Irebi c.1160. 'Irishman' probably referred to a Norse settler who had migrated from Ireland.

**Irton:** The farmstead by the Rivert Irt. Irt + O.E. tūn (see under River Irt—page 22).

**Kelsick:** The ditch where there is a spring. O.N. kelda + O.N. sík. Keldesik 1294.

**Kendal:** Formerly known as 'Kirkby Kendal'—'the village with a church in the valley of the River Kent.' O.N. kirkja + O.N. býr + O.N. dalr (see under River Kent—page 22). Cherkaby Kendale c.1095.

**Keswick:** The cheese farm. O.E. cēse + O.E. wīc. Kesewic 1240. Chesewyk 1285. The 'K' at the beginning of the name is the result of Norse influence on an Old English word.

**Lanthwaite. Loagthwaite:** Both these names mean 'the long clearing: O.N. langr + O.N. thveit. Langthwaite 1505, Longthwayte c.1540.

**Legburthwaite:** The clearing on Leggr's hill or by Leggr's stronghold. O.N. personal name + O.N. berg or borg + O.N. thveit. Legburgthwayte 1530.

**Levens:** Leofa's headland or the leafy headland. O.N. personal name, Leofa or O.N. lauf + O.N. nes. Lefnes c.1170.

**Limefitt:** The water meadow where flax is grown. O.N. lín + O.N. fit. Lynfit c.1170. An alternative derivation from O.N. lím + O.N. fit may also be possible. This would mean 'the muddy meadow'.

**Lindale:** The valley where lime trees grow. O.N. lind + O.N. dalr. Lindale 1246.

**Lorton:** The farm by the roaring stream; or Hlóra's farmstead. O.E. hlōra or O.N. personal name, Hlóra + O.E. tūn. Hlóra is a female figure in Norse mythology whose name also appears in the Norwegian river-name, Lora. Loretuna 1171.

**Lowick:** The leafy hollow. O.N. lauf + O.N. vík. Vík usually refers to a coastal inlet. Here, apparently, it is used to describe the valley of the River Crake. Lofwik 1202.

**Lund:** The grove. O.N. lúndr. Lunds 1578.

**Manesty:** Mani's path. O.N. personal name, Mani, + O.N. stígr. Manistie 1564.

**Meathop:** The middle of the valley. O.E. middel + O.E. hōp. Midhop 1184. The modern form is derived from O.N. mithr rather than O.E. middel.

**Mosser:** The shieling on the peat moss. O.N. mosi + O.N. erg. Mosergh 1279.

**Muncaster:** Muli's fort or Mula's fort. An O.E. or an O.N. personal name + O.E. cæster (from Latin castrum). Muncaster was a Roman fort taken over by later settlers. Mulcastre c.1140.

**Newby Bridge:** This name first appears on Saxton's map in 1577 and probably refers to the builder of the bridge.

**Nibthwaite:** The clearing by the new farmstead. O.N. nýr + O.N. búth + O.N. thveit. Neuburthwait 1336. In 1202 a nearby place-name, now lost, appears as Thornebuthwait, the clearing by the old farmstead, from O.N. forn + O.N. búth + O.N. thveit.

**Ormathwaite:** The Northman's clearing (Northman = Norseman). O.N. personal name + O.N. thveit. Northmanethwait c.1260. The name Northman survived until the 14th century and was replaced by Norman.

**Penny Hill:** This is named after the Penny family who were well-known in the Furness area from the 16th century, cf. Penny Bridge by the River Crake.

**Penrith:** The chief or main ford (over the River Eamont). Welsh 'pen' (in the sense of chief) + Welsh 'rhyd'. Penred 1167. (This interpretation accepts the difficulty that the crossing of the Eamont is at least a mile from Penrith, but the other meaning of 'pen', a hill, does not help to meet this geographical point.)

**Penruddock:** This may have the same meaning as Penrith with a diminutive of 'rhyd'—redoc—as the second element. A possible alternative is that 'pen' here is used in the sense of 'a hill' and that the second element is Welsh 'rhuddawc', red, with an implied reference to the reddish soil in this vicinity. Penruddoc 1292.

**Pooley Bridge:** This was formerly known as Pool How, the hill by the pool or stream. O.E. pōl/O.N. póllr + O.N. haugr. Pulhoue 1252.

**Portinscale:** The harlot's hut. O.E. portcwene + O.N. skáli. Porqeneschal c.1160.

**Ravenglass:** The land given to or belonging to a man named Glas. Gaelic rann-gleis. Renglas C.1208.

**Redmain:** The stony ford. Welsh rhyd + Welsh maen. Redemane 1291.

**Rosgill:** The ravine where horses go. O.N. hross + O.N. gil. Rossegill c.1195.

**Rosthwaite:** The clearing with the heap of stones. O.N. hreysi + O.N. thveit. Raisthwat 1564.

**Watendlath, a distinctive place-name for which no entirely satisfactory explanation has been suggested. Its possible origins are detailed on page 46**

**Rusland:** Hrolfr's land. O.N. personal name + O.N. land. Rolesland 1336.

**Ruthwaite:** The rough clearing. O.E. rūh + O.N. thveit. Ruthwayt 1256.

**Rydal:** The valley where rye is grown. O.E. ryge/O.N. rugr + O.N. dalr/O.E. dæl. Ridale 1180.

**Sadgill:** The gill (or ravine) where the mountain pastures are. O.N. sætr + O.N. gil. Sategill 1279.

**Sandwick:** The sandy inlet. O.N. sand + O.N. vík. Sandwic 1200.

**Santon Bridge:** The bridge by the sandy farmstead. O.E. sand + O.E. tūn. Santon c.1235 (the 'bridge' appears in the 17th century). Not far from Santon is the only sandpit in the area which produces silver-sand.

**Satterthwaite:** The clearing for the summer pastures. O.N. sætr + O.N. thveit. Saterthwayt 1336.

**Sawrey:** The muddy places. O.N. saurar (plural) Sourer 1336. Near and Far Sawrey lie in a small valley between Esthwaite Water and Lake Windermere, a low-lying area which may well have been especially wet at one time.

**Seathwaite** (Borrowdale): The clearing among the sedges. O.N. sef + O.N. thveit. Seuthwayt 1340.

**Seathwaite** (Duddon Valley): The clearing near the lake (i.e. Seathwaite Tarn). O.N. sær + O.N. thveit. Seathwot 1592.

**Seatoller:** Either: the summer pastures among the alder bushes, O.N. alor + O.N. sætr; or: Olvar's summer shieling, O.N. personal name + O.N. sætr. An inversion compound—see page 13. Seataller 1566.

**Setmurthy:** Murdoch's summer shieling. An old Irish surname, Murdoch, + O.N. sætr. An inversion compound—see page 13. Satmerdoc 1195. A Stephano Murdoc appears here in a 12th century record.

**Shap:** The heap of stones (probably the ruins of a Stone Circle). O.E. hēap. Hep c.1175. The additional 's' in front of the 'h' of the early form 'Hep' is an unusual linguistic development which may also be found in the name Shoulthwaite.

**Shoulthwaite:** The clearing where the (mill)wheel stands. O.N. hjól + O.N. thveit. Heolthwaitis c.1280. The mill was probably built on Naddle Beck.

**Sizergh:** Sigrid's shieling. O.N. feminine personal name Sigrithr + O.N. erg. Sigaritherge 1170.

**Skelwith:** This was originally 'Schelwath' which means 'the noisy ford' probably referring to the waterfall near to a crossing of the River Brathay. When the bridge was built the ford or 'wath' was forgotten and the name assumed its present form. O.N. skjallr + O.N. vath. Schelwath 1246. The waterfall is now known as Skelwith Force: O.N. fors.

**Smaithwaite:** The smooth or level clearing. O.E. smethe + O.N.

thveit. Smetwayt 1245.

**Smeathwaite:** The small or narrow clearing. O.N. smá + O.N. thveit. Smathwaitis c.1280.

**Snittlegarth:** The enclosure where snares are set. The first element is the dialect word 'snittle', a snare, usually of the noose type; + O.N. garthr. Snittlegarth 1608.

**Soulby:** Sula's farmstead. Sula is an old Danish feminine name; + O.Dan. by. Suleby c.1160.

**Stair:** No early forms are available, but it is possible that a reference is intended to the steep rise in the road at this point. If so, the derivation could be the O.E. stæger, to climb, from which the word 'stair' derives. Stayre 1565.

**Stang End:** This is probably derived from O.N. stong, a post, usually indicating a boundary mark or the limits of a measured piece of land.

**Stanger:** See Stang End. The second element here is O.N. rá, a boundary mark, thus giving the meaning 'a post which marks a specific boundary'. Stangre 1298.

**Staveley:** The woodland clearing where staves are found. O.E. stæf + O.E. lēah. Stafleia 1235.

**Stonethwaite:** The stony clearing. O.N. steinn + O.N. thveit. Stainthwait 1211.

**Strands:** The bank of the river (Irt). O.E. strand. Strand of Irt 1578.

**Swinside:** The summer pasture or shieling where pigs are kept. O.N. svín + O.N. sætr. Swynesate 1242. The element 'sate' in the early form (derived from O.N. sætr has been replaced by 'side' in the modern name, cf. Ambleside.

**Thackthwaite:** The clearing where reeds for thatching grow. O.N. thak + O.N. thveit. Thacthwaite 1220.

**Thirlspot:** The giant's pool. O.N. thurs/O.E. thyrs + M.E. potte/ O.N. pot. Thirspott 1616. The additional 'l' may have developed by association with Thirlmere nearby which has quite a different origin (see Thirlmere—page 17).

**Thornthwaite. Thornythwaite:** The clearing with the thornbushes. O.N. thorn + O.N. thveit. Thornethwayt 1230.

**Threlkeld:** The thrall's spring. O.N. thræll + O.N. kelda. Trellekeld 1278. The term 'thrall' (serf or slave) seems to have been used by the Norse settlers to describe the native Britons.

**Tilberthwaite:** The clearing by Tilli's fort. O.E. personal name + O.E. burh + O.N. thveit. Tildesburgthwait 1196. Slight remains of an early stronghold may still be seen here. Tilberthwaite.

**Torver:** Several interpretations of this name have been put forward, all based on the same Norse origins. (i) The shieling with a turf roof; (ii) the shieling where peat is cut or stacked; (iii) Torfi's shieling. O.N. torf (or O.N. personal name, Torfi) + O.N. erg.

**Troutbeck:** The trout stream. O.E. trūht + O.N. bekkr. Trutebec 1179.

**Ulcat Row:** The nook of land with the cottage where owls have their haunt. O.E. ūle/O.N. ugla + O.E. cot/O.N. kot + O.N. vrá. Ulcotewra c.1250.

**Uldale:** The valley of the wolves. O.N. úlfr + O.N. dalr. Ulvesdal c.1216.

**Ullock:** The place where the wolves play. O.N. úlfr + O.N. leikr. Ulvelaik 1279.

**Ulpha:** The wolf's hill. O.N. úlfr + O.N. haugr. Ulfhou 1337.

**Ullthwaite:** The clearing haunted by wolves. O.N. ulfr + O.N. thveit. Ulvethwayt 1301.

**Ulverston:** Wulfhere's or Ulfr's farmstead. O.E. or O.N. personal name + O.E. tūn. Ulureston 1086.

**Uzzicar:** The cultivated field with a dwellinghouse. O.E. hūs + O.E. æcer. Husaker 1210. An acre was a piece of cultivated land of varying size before it became a precise measurement (with local variations) by The Statute for Measuring Land of 1284.

**Waberthwaite:** The clearing with the hunting or fishing hut. O.N. veithi + O.N. búth + O.N. thveit. Waythebutwayth c.1210.

**Watendlath:** No entirely satisfactory explanation of this name has so far been suggested. Early forms vary so widely as to be of little guidance. The most acceptable suggestions are: (i) That the first two elements are derived from O.N. vatn and O.N. endi with the final element possibly derived from O.N. hlatha. This would give a meaning of 'the barn at the end of the lake'. However, this is regarded by many as linguistically very dubious. (ii) That it is derived from a British personal name such as 'Gwenddoleu' with O.N. vatn added as the first element at a later date. This would then be an inversion compound (see page 13), meaning 'Gwenddoleu's lake'. To the newly arrived Norse settlers such an unfamiliar personal name would inevitably lead to strange contortions as they attempted to pronounce it and this may account for the remarkable version which appeared in 1211—'Wathenthendelan'.

**Watermillock:** The little hill where wethers graze. Welsh meloc + O.E. wether. Wethermeloc c.1215.

**Whelpo:** The hill of the cubs. O.N. hvelpr + O.N. haugr. Whelphowe 1333.

**Winster:** The left-hand side (river). O.N. vinstri. Winster c.1180. The name clearly involves a comparison with a 'right-hand side' and it seems likely this refers to the River Leven which flows southwards to form the western (or right-hand) boundary of the district of Cartmel as the Winster forms the eastern (or left-hand) boundary. An interesting alternative has been suggested that the name Winster might be identified with the Welsh name Gwensteri, the site of a battle described in the Book of Taliesin. The derivation then would be from the Welsh gwyn + ster, the white river.

**Witherslack:** The wooded hollow. O.N. vithr + O.N. slakki. Witherslak 1186.

**Wray:** A secluded nook or corner of land. O.N. vrá. Wraye c.1535.

**Wythburn:** The valley where willow trees grow. O.E. withig + O.E. botm. Wythbottune c.1280. The second element was changed to 'burn' in the 17th century.

**Wythop:** The valley where willow trees grow. O.E. withig + O.E. hōp. Wythope 1279.

**Yanwath:** The flat or level woodland. O.E. efn + O.E. wudu, later changed to O.N. jafn + O.N. vithr. Euenwith c.1150. Yafnewid c.1245. (This is Ekwall's explanation of a complex name in which the element 'wath' (a ford) is obviously inappropriate and must be a later change totally inconsistent with the early forms of the name.)

**Boot—the sheepfold or the bend in the valley**

47

# Other place-names of special interest

**Adelaide Hill:** Formerly known as 'Oakbank' this famous viewpoint by Lake Windermere was renamed following a visit by Queen Adelaide in 1840. She also gave her name to Adelaide, the capital of South Australia.

**Belle Isle:** Formerly known as 'Longholme' this island in Windermere was renamed after its purchase by Isabella Curwen in 1781.

**Black Sail:** This is 'the dark stream' from O.N. blakkr + O.N. seyla. The stream joins the River Liza in Ennerdale and in 1322 was known as Le Blacksayl.

**Borrans:** Several places bear this or a similar name. It is derived from O.E. burgæsn, a burial mound, but almost any ancient heap of stones may acquire the name.

**Bowder Stone:** This 2,000 ton mass of rock in Borrowdale was deposited in its present precarious position by the melting ice some 12,000 years ago. Its name is the dialect term for a large boulder derived from M.E. bulder-stān.

**Brockhole:** Formerly the home of Manchester businessman William Henry Gaddum, Brockhole is now the National Park Centre and, appropriately, has the badger as its symbol, for it is derived from O.E. brocc-hōl, the badger's hollow.

**Copeland:** This was one of the baronial forests of Cumbria and its name probably originated in a land transaction of the Norse settlements. It means 'the bought land' and was known in 1125 as Caupalandia—O.N. kaupaland.

**Copperheap Bay:** Copper ore was taken by boat from this point on the shore of Derwentwater from the mines in Newlands to the smelting works at Brigham near Keswick.

**Cumberland:** The county name disappeared in 1974 with the revival of the name of Cumbria which appears in the year 945 as 'Cumbraland'—'the land of the Cymru'.

**Doctor's Bridge:** This packhorse bridge in Eskdale was widened in 1734 by Dr. Edward Tyson to allow his carriage to pass over. His alterations can be seen under the arch of the bridge.

**Dunmail Raise:** Here, according to tradition, is the grave of Dunmail, one of the last kings of Strathclyde, allegedly killed in battle against Edmund, King of the Saxons, in 945. In fact, Dunmail survived the battle and died in Rome 30 years later. Even so, the name means 'Dunmail's cairn'. O.N. hreysi.

**Flaska:**  The flat wood. O.N. flatr + O.N. skógr. Flatscogh 1278. Flaska Common was stripped of its forest at an early date and its peat mosses were extensively cut as fuel for the smelting furnaces at Brigham, near Keswick, during the late 16th and early 17th centuries.

**Friar's Crag:**  This famous promontory on the shore of Derwentwater is traditionally the spot where St. Cuthbert parted from St. Herbert at their last meeting (see St. Herbert's Isle—page 51). The term 'friar' here means 'brother' in the monastic sense.

**Furness:**  This name appears in 1150 as Futhernessa which suggests a derivation from an O.N. personal name, Futh (Futhar is the possessive form) + O.N. nes = Futh's headland. Originally the name referred only to the headland now known as Rampside Point, and Peel island opposite was known as Futh's Island. Only much later was Furness applied to the areas of High and Low Furness.

**Garburn:**  The stream in the gore. O.N. burna + O.E. gāra. A gore is a triangular piece of land and here it refers to a projection into the parish of Kentmere.

**Goldscope:**  This is a corruption of the German 'Gottes Gab' or God's Gift. The name was given by jubilant German miners to the rich vein of copper and lead which they discovered in this mine after months of searching (1566).

**Goody Bridge:**  This, like many other Lakeland bridges, was almost certainly named after the man who built it. Guddy Brig 1586.

**Gowder Crag:**  The distinct echo for which this Borrowdale crag is famous gave it its name. The 1338 version, Gauth Crag, is derived from O.N. gauth meaning 'barking', here used in the sense of an echo: 'the echoing crag'.

**Gowk Hill:**  Cuckoo hill. O.N. gaukr. Gowk is still used in northern dialect for a cuckoo.

**'Ground':**  Numerous Lakeland farms are called 'Grounds': for example Roger Ground, Kitchen Ground, Brocklebank Ground, Stephenson Ground, Jackson Ground, Carter Ground, etc. The term refers to land which was part of monastic estates and was sold at the Dissolution as individual holdings. The name preceding 'Ground' is usually that of the family who acquired the land at that time.

**Hardknott Pass:**  This is a fairly modern name borrowed from nearby Hardknott Fell. The pass was formerly known as Wainscarth derived from O.E. wægen, a waggon, and from O.N. skarth, a pass. 'Wainscarth' was, therefore, 'a pass along which a wain or waggon could be taken'.

**Harry Guards Wood:**  The wood with the grey, lichen-covered enclosures. O.N. hárr + O.N. garthr. In the absence of early forms this explanation may be inferred from the presence of ancient stone enclosures here: how ancient it is impossible to say.

**Honister:**   No early forms are available to give guidance on this name. A possible interpretation is based on a Norwegian place-name, Hunastad or 'Huni's place'. The final element could be O.N. stathr or O.N. sætr.

**Hunting Stile:**   A late 19th century version—'Hunting Sty'—would suggest that this is 'the path taken by the hunt', derived from O.N. stígr or O.E. stigel.

**Inglewood:**   This was the largest Royal Forest in England, extending forty miles from Cross Fell to the Solway and twenty-five miles from north to south. It was 'the forest of the Angles', from O.E. Engla + O.E. wudu.

**Kirkstone:**   A large boulder near the summit of Kirkstone Pass is said to resemble a church, but the name 'kirk' was often given to many unexplained heaps of stones in the belief that they had some supernatural or religious significance. Tröllakirkja in Iceland— 'the trolls' church'—acquired its name in this way. The 1184 version of Kirkstone—Kirkestain—clearly indicates a Norse origin from O.N. kirkja + O.N. steinn.

**Lady's Rake:**   A 'rake'—O.N. reik—is a path up a hillside along which animals were taken to summer pastures. This particular 'rake' is, according to tradition, the path by which the Countess of Derwentwater escaped after the arrest of her husband for his part in the Jacobite Rebellion of 1715 (see Lord's Island).

**Lodore Falls:**   Lodore is the 'low door' or gap in the ridge through which Watendlath Beck pours to form the famous waterfall. The origin of the name is clearly indicated by the 1210 version— Laghedure from O.N. lágr + O.E. duru.

**Lord's Island:**   This island in Derwentwater was formerly known as Wytholm (1317) or 'the island of willow trees'. It acquired its present name when the Radcliffe family, Earls of Derwentwater, built their residence there. The Radcliffe Estates were given to Greenwich Hospital following the Earl's execution for his part in the 1715 Jacobite Rebellion.

**Lyulph's Tower:**   This well-known landmark by Ullswater was built and named by the Duke of Norfolk in the 18th century. Lyulph was Ligulf, an ancestor of the Barons of Greystoke.

**Mickleden:**   This valley forms an upper branch of the long, broad valley of Great Langdale and its name is derived from O.E. miceldenu, the big valley.

**Moses' Trod:**   This is a pathway (or 'trod' in local dialect) which runs from the Wasdale flank of Great Gable along the side of the fell to just below Wind Gap and then on to Green Gable, Brand-reth and so to Honister Hause. Moses, so the story goes, was a quarryman who smuggled Borrowdale wad by this route to the

50

coast at Ravenglass when he exchanged it for tobacco and rum. His own privately distilled whisky also formed part of what must have been a tough, risky but no doubt profitable business in contraband goods.

**Nan Bield:** A 'bield' (M.E. belde) is a hut or shelter or an animal's den and in Lakeland place-names it is usually preceded by the name of an animal—e.g. Fox Bield, Otter Bield, Goose Bield, etc. In this case the interpretation is more difficult since 'Nan' is usually a pet form of the feminine name Ann and the obvious explanation of Nan Bield is 'Ann's hut or shelter'.

**Neaum Hurst:** A 'hurst' is a wooded hillside (O.E. hyrst) and 'neaum' is the name of a type of slate found in the local quarries. There were three types of slates produced here: London, County and Neaum Tom.

**Ore Gap:** 'The pass where iron ore is found': a reference to the ancient iron workings found near this spot. They may date from the mining activities of the monks of Furness Abbey who are known to have worked the ores in Eskdale and to have had a smelting furnace or bloomery in Langstrath. Orscard 1242 = O.E. ōra + O.N. skarth.

**Ritson Force:** This waterfall on the Mosedale Beck near Wasdale Head commemorates Will Ritson who lived at Row Foot from 1808 to 1890 and became famous as innkeeper, mountain guide, raconteur and friend of academics, poets and bishops.

**St. Herbert's Isle:** This island of Derwentwater is traditionally said to have been the home of the 7th century hermit, St. Herbert, the close friend of St. Cuthbert of Lindisfarne.

**Sampson's Bratful:** This huge mound on Stockdale Moor, 96 feet long and 6 feet high, may be a vast cairn marking an ancient burial site, but it still retains its secrets as it has not yet been excavated. The legend is that the Devil carried all the stones here in his 'brat' or apron and dumped them. Sampson is unexplained.

**Scale Force:** The shieling by the waterfall. O.N. skáli + O.N. fors. Scale Force is Lakeland's most impressive waterfall, 125 feet high: 'a slender stream faintly illuminating a gloomy fissure' (Wordsworth).

**Scots' Rake:** A rake (O.N. reik) is a path up a hillside used to drive animals to summer pastures. This path is part of the Roman road which runs over High Street and it probably acquired its present name when it was used by Scottish raiders during the troubled times in the north of England in the 14th century.

**Slater Bridge:** This unusual bridge across the River Brathay near Little Langdale Tarn is constructed of large slabs of slate and is believed to have been built by the quarrymen to enable them to cross the river dryshod (the alternative was the nearby ford) on their way to work in the great slate quarries at Tilberthwaite and Hodge Close. E.P.N.S., however, states unequivocally that the name derives from the family of John Sleyther referred to in the Kendal records from the 1390s.

**Spoon Hall:** The O.E. word 'spōn' means a wood-chipping such as might be used for roof shingles; and 'hall' has replaced 'how' as in many other place-names in this area. The 1690 form—Spoonhow—indicates a derivation from O.E. spōn and O.N. haugr. Spoon Hall therefore was 'the hill where roof shingles are found'.

**Stake Pass. Sticks Pass:** Both these names refer to the poles or stakes which were used to mark the path over the passes.

**Stockley Bridge:** The bridge on the path to Styhead from Borrowdale stands in what was once a woodland clearing. The word 'stockley' is derived from O.E. stocc, a tree stump, and O.E. lēah, a woodland clearing. As much of the district was heavily wooded until the later Middle Ages, this seems more probable than the present scene might suggest.

**Styhead Pass:** This means 'the pass at the highest point on the path up the hill' and it is derived from O.E. stīg + O.E. hēafod. It was formerly known as Hederlanghals (1209), a more difficult name to analyse. 'Lang' is O.N. langr, long, and 'hals' is O.N. meaning 'a pass', but 'heder' is obscure: it is unlikely to be 'heather' as some suggest, but it may be O.E. ǣdre which implies a rapidly flowing stream. So the original name might mean 'the long path over the pass by the rapidly flowing stream'.

**Sweden How:** This hillside and the well-known bridge, Sweden Bridge, nearby, have only a linguistic connection with Scandinavia: 'sweden' is O.N. 'svíthinn', land clearing by burning; and 'how' is O.N. haugr, a hill. Swythene 1274.

**Tenter Howe:** The many place-names which contain the term 'tenter' are a reminder of the fact that for many centuries the textile industry was a major part of the economy of the Lake District. A tenter is a wooden frame on which cloth was stretched after fulling (cleansing) to prevent it from shrinking. A 'tenter how' was a hillside on which tenter frames were erected: cf. the phrase 'to be on tenter hooks'.

**The Screes:** This name is given to the impressive cascade of fragmented stone and shattered rock which forms the steep slopes on the southern shore of Wastwater. It is referred to in 1537 as Scrithes Edge. O.N. skritha, a landslip.

**Throstle Garth:** Two very different interpretations of this name have been put forward. The first accepts 'throstle' as a direct reference to the song-thrush. With O.N. garthr this would result in 'the song-thrush's enclosure'. Similar names in other parts of the north country suggest that 'throstle' is not derived from O.N. trosla, a song thrush, but from an O.N. personal name, Frosthildr. The meaning then would be 'Frosthildr's enclosure'.

**Tottling Stone:** This 9 feet high boulder by Launchy Gill in the woods by Thirlmere was probably left in its apparently precarious position by the melting ice. Its name is derived from the Cumbrian dialect verb 'to tottle' meaning to be unsteady or liable to topple over.

**Westmorland:**   This former county name disappeared in 1974 and it originally referred to 'the land of the people living west of the moors', a description which must have been given by the people on the eastern side: i.e. those who lived on the other side of the Pennines. Westmoringaland c. 1150.

**Wrynose Pass:**   This name has caused much controversy. An early interpretation, still widely accepted, was that it is derived from O.N. vreini, a stallion, as might be inferred from the 1157 version 'Wreineshals'. Linguistic objections to this interpretation have resulted in an alternative analysis in which the first element 'Wreineshals' is O.N. vrangr (O.E. writhan and M.E. wreyne) meaning 'twisting', and the second element is O.N. nes, a spur of land; the third is O.N. hals, a pass. This analysis results in 'the pass over the twisting spur of land', no doubt referring to the convoluted nature of the fell landscape over which the route winds its way up to the pass. The 'hals' or actual col is the watershed between the River Brathay and the River Duddon.

**Slater Bridge, Little Langdale, referring either to the quarrymen who worked at the Tilberthwaite and Hodge Close slate quarries or to the family of John Sleyther.**

# Glossary

| | | |
|---|---|---|
| á | ON | a river |
| æcer/akr | OE/ON | a cultivated piece of land |
| æppel/epli | OE/ON | an apple (tree) |
| æsc | OE | an ash tree |
| ald | OE | old |
| alor/elri | OE/ON | alder bushes |
| á-mot | OE | a confluence of rivers |
| austr | ON | east |
| | | |
| bākstān | ME | a flat stone such as bread could be baked on |
| band | ME | the ridge of a hill |
| báss | ON | a cowshed |
| bēam | OE | a tree trunk |
| beinvithr | ON | a holly tree (literally 'bone-wood') |
| bekkr | ON | a stream, a beck |
| belde | ME | a bield or shelter, an animal's den |
| beorg/berg | OE/ON | a hill, a mountain |
| bere | OE | barley |
| bield | dial. | a shelter, an animal's den (see 'belde') |
| birki | ON | birch trees |
| bjalli | ON | a round or bell-shaped hill |
| bjork | ON | a birch tree |
| blá | ON | dark, deep blue |
| blaec/blakkr | OE/ON | black |
| blaen | Welsh | a top, a summit |
| bleikr | ON | a light or pale colour |
| blind | OE/ON | having no outlet, hidden, overgrown |
| boga/bogi | OE/ON | a bend (in a river or valley); bow-shaped |
| borg | ON | a fort |
| bōth | ODan | a hut or herdsman's cottage |
| bōtl | OE | a house, a dwelling |
| botm/botn | OE/ON | a low-lying place, a depression, valley bottom |
| bought | dial. | a sheepfold |
| bouzht | ME | a bend (in a river or valley) |
| braken | ME | bracken |
| brame | ME | a bramble or blackberry |
| brant | OE | steep |
| breithr | ON | broad, wide |
| brekka | ON | a hill or slope |
| brende/brent | OE/ON | burned |
| brōc | OE | a brook |
| brocc/brokkr | OE/ON | a badger |
| brycg/bryggja | OE/ON | a bridge |
| bú | ON | a homestead |
| bucc/bukkr | OE/ON | a buck |
| bucca/bokki | OE/ON | a he-goat |
| bula | OE | a bull |
| bulder-stān | OE | a large boulder, a boulderstone |
| búr | ON | a storehouse |
| būr | OE | a herdsman's cottage |
| burgæsn | OE | a burial place |
| burh | OE | a fortified place |
| burna | OE | a stream |
| buskr | ON | a bush |

54

| | | |
|---|---|---|
| butere | OE | butter |
| búth | ON | a hut, a bothy |
| bȳ | ODan | an isolated farmstead, a village, a hamlet |
| bygg | ON | barley |
| býr | ON | an isolated farmstead, a village, a hamlet |
| bȳre | OE | a byre, a cowshed |
| | | |
| cæster | OE | a walled fortress (from Latin castrum) |
| cald/kaldr | OE/ON | cold |
| caled | Welsh | rapid, rocky, (of a stream) |
| calf/kalfr | OE/ON | a calf |
| camb | OE | a crest or ridge |
| carrec | OWelsh | a rock |
| castel | OE | a castle or fort (from Latin castellum) |
| cateir | Welsh | a chair |
| catt/kattr | OE/ON | a wild-cat |
| caucie | OFr | a causeway or raised road |
| cawm | Welsh | a reed |
| cempe | OE | a warrior |
| cēse | OE | cheese |
| clapper | ME | a rough bridge of large stones |
| clif/klif | OE/ON | a very steep slope or hillside |
| cokelayk | ME | a place where birds play (? a mating dance) |
| col | OE | charcoal |
| cot | OE | a cottage |
| crəgge | ME | a crag |
| creic* | Br | a rock |
| cringol* | OE | wrinkled, twisted |
| cros | OE | a cross |
| crumbāco* | Br | crooked |
| cumb/cwm | OE/Welsh | a valley (usually on the flank of a hill) |
| cunētio* | Br | a sacred stream |
| Cymry | Welsh | the Welsh people (applied to the Cumbrian people) |
| cyning | OE | a king |
| | | |
| dæl | OE | a dale or valley |
| dakru* | Br | a teardrop |
| dalr | ON | a valley or dale |
| deigr | Welsh | a teardrop |
| denu | OE | a narrow wooded valley, a dene |
| derw* | Br | an oak tree |
| derwentio* | Br | abounding in oak trees |
| djúp | ON | deep |
| docce | OE | dock, sorrel, water-lily |
| dodde | ME | a rounded hill usually bare or grassy |
| drag/dreg | ON | a place where boats must be dragged, a portage |
| dub | dial. | a deep pool, a pond |
| dubaco | OWelsh | the dark one |
| dubro* | Br | a stream, a river |
| dúfa | ON | a dove or pigeon |
| dun | Gael | a hill-fort, a stronghold |
| dor/doru | OE | a door or gap |
| dwfr | Welsh | a stream a river |
| dyr | ON | a deer |
| | | |
| ēa | OE | a river |
| earn | OE | an eagle |
| ēast | OE | east |
| efn | OE | flat; level, even |

| | | |
|---|---|---|
| eik | ON | oak |
| elptr | ON | a swan |
| elri | ON | alder bushes |
| endi | ON | the end |
| eng | ON | a meadow or outlying pasture |
| Engla | OE | of the Angles |
| ēowu | OE | a ewe |
| epli | ON | an apple (tree) |
| erg | ON | a shieling, an outlying pasture |
| ermite | ME | a hermit |
| esk | OWelsh | water |
| eski | ON | an ash-tree |
| ey | ON | a small island, a water meadow |
| eyrr | ON | a gravel bank |
| | | |
| fæger/fagr | OE/ON | fair, pleasant |
| fald | OE | a fold |
| féhús | ON | a cattle shed |
| fjall | ON | a fell, a mountain |
| fit | ON | a meadow, especially a water-meadow |
| flatr | ON | flat, level |
| flói/flow | ON/dial. | an open peat-bog, a watery moss |
| ford | OE | a ford |
| forn | ON | old |
| fors | ON | a waterfall, a force |
| fūl/fúll | OE/ON | muddy, dirty |
| fyrthe | OE | a wood |
| | | |
| gafl | ON | a gable |
| gāra | OE | a gore or wedge-shaped piece of land |
| garthr | ON | an enclosure, a farmyard |
| gás | ON | a goose |
| gāt | OE | a goat |
| gata | ON | a road, a path |
| gaukr | ON | a cuckoo |
| gauth | ON | barking, 'echoing' |
| geat | OE | a gate |
| geit | ON | a goat |
| gemot | OE | a meeting place |
| gil | ON | a narrow ravine (later the stream in the 'gill') |
| gildri | ON | a snare, a trap |
| gliúfr | ON | a ravine |
| glyn | Welsh | a wooded valley, a glen |
| gnípa | ON | a steep rock |
| gol | ON | the wind |
| golde | OE | the marigold, the kingcup |
| gōs | OE | a goose |
| græg | OE | grey |
| græs/gres | OE/ON | grass |
| grange | ME/Fr | an outlying farm (usually of a monastery) |
| grein | ON | the fork in a valley where streams meet |
| grēne | OE | green |
| grēot/grjót | OE/ON | grave, stone, small rocks |
| griss | ON | a pig |
| gwyn | Welsh | white |
| gylping | OE/OWel | a gushing stream |
| gymbr | ON | a yearling sheep, a gimmer |
| | | |
| hæg/hagi | OE/ON | an enclosure, usually for hunting purposes |
| hafri | ON | oats |

56

| | | |
|---|---|---|
| halh | OE | a secluded nook of land (often by a river) |
| hals | ON | a narrow pass, a col, a 'hause' |
| hár | ON | high |
| hār | OE | a boundary (from an association with landmarks) |
| hara | OE | a hare |
| hárr | ON | hoary, covered with lichen |
| harthr | ON | rough, rocky, hard |
| haugr | ON | a hill, a 'how' |
| haukr | ON | a hawk |
| hēafod | OE | the highest part of a hill, a headland |
| hēah | OE | high |
| hēap | OE | a heap of stones |
| heorot | OE | a hart |
| hestr | ON | a horse |
| hind | OE/ON | a hind |
| hjálmr | ON | a helmet, a cattle-shelter |
| hjól | ON | a wheel |
| hjortr | ON | a hart |
| hlatha | ON | a barn |
| hlóra | OE | a roaring (stream) |
| hofuth | ON | the highest part of a hill, a headland |
| hōh | OE | a ridge, a spur |
| hōl/holr | OE/ON | a hole or hollow |
| holegn | OE | holly |
| holmr | ON | an island or land almost surrounded by water |
| hōp/hóp | OE/ON | a small valley |
| how | dial. | a small hill, a knoll, a mound (from ON haugr) |
| hrafn | ON | a raven |
| hramsa | ON | wild garlic |
| hreysi | ON | a cairn or large heap of stones |
| hrjóstr | ON | rough, rugged |
| hross | ON | a horse |
| hrycg/hryggr | OE/ON | a ridge, usually with steep slopes |
| hūs/hús | OE/ON | a house |
| hvelpr | ON | a whelp, a cub |
| hvin* | ON | furze, gorse |
| hvitr | ON | white |
| hyll | OE | a hill |
| hylr | ON | a pool |
| hyrst | OE | a copse, a wooded hillside |
| | | |
| ikorni | ON | a squirrel |
| illr | ON | steep; also evil, malevolent |
| ingas | OE | the people who live at ... |
| intak | ON | land enclosed from waste, intake land |
| ir | Welsh | fresh, green |
| Iri | ON | belonging to the Irishmen (i.e. Norse settlers) |
| | | |
| jafn | ON | flat, level, even |
| | | |
| kampi | ON | a warrior |
| kartr* | ON | rough or rocky ground |
| kattr | ON | a wild-cat |
| kaupaland | ON | land acquired by purchase; 'bought' land |
| kelda | ON | a spring, a 'well' |
| kerling | ON | an old woman, a witch |
| kide | ME | a kid, a young goat |
| kirkja | ON | a church |
| kith | ON | a kid, a young goat |

| | | |
|---|---|---|
| kjarr | ON | a marsh |
| kleif | ON | a steep slope |
| knútr | ON | a craggy hill, a rocky outcrop |
| kol | ON | charcoal |
| konungr | ON | a king |
| kot | ON | a cottage, a hut |
| kra | ON | a corner |
| krókr | ON | a crook or bend (in a river) |
| kross | ON | a cross |
| kukrā* | Br | crooked |
| kvi | ON | a fold or shelter for animals |
| | | |
| læfer | OE | reedy, rushy |
| lād | OE | a vein of ore, a lode |
| lágr | ON | low |
| langr | ON | long |
| látr | ON | an animal's lair |
| lauf | ON | leafy |
| lauthr | ON | foam, lather |
| lēah | OE | a clearing in a wood, a meadow |
| leikr | ON | play |
| lettir | Gael | a slope |
| līm | OE | lime (a sticky substance) |
| līn/lin | OE/ON | flax |
| lind | ON | a lime-tree |
| liwcyl* | Br | bright, shining |
| ljós | ON | light, shining |
| llyfyn | Welsh | smooth |
| loch | Gael | a lake |
| lumme | OE | a pool |
| lundr | ON | a grove, a small wood |
| lykkja | ON | a curve or loop |
| lyng | ON | heather, ling |
| | | |
| maen | Welsh | stony |
| mallacht | Gael | cursed |
| mathra | ON | the madder plant |
| meigh* | Br | to urinate, to drizzle |
| meloc | Welsh | a little hill |
| melr | ON | a sandhill, a sandbank |
| mēre | OE | a lake or pool |
| micel/mikill | OE/ON | large, great |
| middel | OE | middle |
| mimeto* | Br | noise |
| mithr | ON | middle |
| moel | Welsh | a hill, usually round and grassy |
| mōr | OE | moorland, wasteland |
| mos/mosi | OE/ON | moss, peat, peat-bog, marsh |
| (ge) mot | OE | a meeting or meeting-place |
| mýrr | ON | a marsh, mire, swampy ground |
| | | |
| nabbi | ON | a projecting spur, usually with a steep fall |
| naddr | ON | a wedge-shaped piece of land or valley |
| nes | ON | a headland or promontory |
| nīwe/nýr | OE/ON | new |
| | | |
| ongul | ON | a fishing hook |
| orn | ON | an eagle |
| orri | ON | a blackcock |
| orrusta | ON | a battle |

| | | |
|---|---|---|
| pen/penno* | Welsh/Br | a top; head, chief, main |
| pīc/pík | OE/ON | a peak, a sharp summit (ON 'pík' is found only in Cumbria) |
| pōl/póllr | OE/ON | a pool or sluggish stream |
| portcwene | OE | a harlot |
| pot/potte | ON/ME | a deep hole, pool or pit |
| | | |
| rá | ON | a boundary mark |
| rann | OIrish | a share (of land) |
| rautande | ON | roaring (present participle of 'rauta') |
| rauthi | ON | the trout |
| rauthr | ON | red |
| rēad | OE | red |
| reik (rák) | ON | a path up a hill, a 'rake' (to take animals to hill pastures) |
| rhedyn | Welsh | bracken |
| rhuddawc | Welsh | red |
| rhyd | Welsh | a ford |
| rigging | ME | a ridge |
| rille | OE | a rill or brook |
| rugr/ryge | ON/OE | rye |
| rūh | OE | rough |
| | | |
| sær | ON | water, lake |
| sætr | ON | hill pastures used in the summer, the shielings built at these pastures; a saeter |
| saur | ON | muddy (plural 'saurar') |
| scēap | OE | sheep |
| sef | ON | sedge |
| seyla | ON | a muddy place; a dark stream |
| sic/sík | OE/ON | a ditch or a drainage channel; a marshy stream |
| sine | dial. | to drain away, to dry up |
| skáli | ON | a hut, usually away from the farm, e.g. at a saeter |
| skalli | ON | bare, bald |
| skammr | ON | short |
| skarth | ON | a gap in a ridge often used of a mountain pass |
| sker | ON | a steep crag or precipice, a scar |
| skith | ON | a billet of wood, firewood |
| skjallr | ON | noisy, resounding (usually of water) |
| skógr | ON | a wood |
| skritha | ON | a landslip, a scree |
| skúti/skót | ON | a rocky projection, a rising bridge |
| skyti | ON | an archer |
| slæd | OE | a valley |
| slakki | ON | a depression or shallow valley |
| sletta | ON | a level pasture or field |
| smá | ON | small, narrow |
| smethe | OE | smooth |
| snittle | dial. | a snare or noose |
| spōn | OE | a wood-chipping such as used for roof shingles |
| spretta | ON | to spurt or gush |
| stæf | OE | a stave |
| stakkr | ON | a pillar of rock, steep rocks |
| stān | OE | stone |
| stang/stong | OE/ON | a pole or stake, often to mark a boundary |
| stede/stathr | OE/ON | the site of a building, a farmstead |
| steinn | ON | a stone |
| steōr | OE | a steer, a young bullock |
| -ster | Welsh | -stream |

| | | |
|---|---|---|
| sticele | OE | a steep place |
| stig/stígr | OE/ON | a steep path, a ladder |
| stigel | OE | a steep path, a high ridge, (later also a stile) |
| stikill | ON | a sharp peak or summit |
| stjórr | ON | a steer, a young bullock |
| stoc | OE | a landholding, a demesne |
| stocc/stokkr | OE/ON | the trunk or stump of a tree |
| stræt | OE | a paved way |
| strand | OE/ON | the shore of a lake, the bank of a stream |
| strōd | OE | marsh overgrown with brushwood |
| sútari/sutere | ON/OE | a cobbler, a shoemaker |
| svartr | ON | dark, black |
| svin | ON | pig, swine |
| svithinn | ON | land cleared by burning |
| | | |
| thak | ON | thatch, i.e. reeds etc. used for thatching |
| thorn | OE/ON | thorn bushes |
| thræl/thrǽll | OE/ON | a thrall, serf or slave |
| thveit | ON | a clearing for pasture |
| thyrel | OE | a hollow |
| thyrs/thurs | OE/ON | a giant (with pagan or supernatural overtones) |
| tjorn | ON | a tarn or small lake |
| torf | ON | turf, cut peat |
| tottle | dial. | to be unsteady, in danger of toppling over |
| trēow/tré | OE/ON | a tree |
| trūht | OE | a trout |
| tūn/tún | OE/ON | a farmstead, an enclosed piece of land, a hamlet |
| tunga | ON | a tongue of land |
| tyri | ON | resinous fir or pine-wood |
| | | |
| ūle/ugla | OE/ON | an owl |
| úlfr | ON | a wolf |
| | | |
| vandr | ON | an osier |
| varthr | ON | a cairn, a heap of stones |
| vath | ON | a ford |
| vatn | ON | a stretch of water, a lake |
| veithr | ON | hunting, fishing |
| vethr | ON | a wether, a castrated ram |
| vík | ON | a creek, an inlet (usually on the coast) |
| vinstri | ON | the left-hand side |
| vithr | ON | a wood |
| vrá | ON | a corner or secluded nook of land, often close to water, swamp or wasteland |
| vrangr | ON | crooked, twisting, convoluted |
| vreini | ON | a stallion |
| | | |
| wæter | OE | water, lake |
| wella | OE | a stream |
| wether | OE | a castrated ram, a wether |
| whinne | ME | furze, gorse |
| wīc | OE | a dairy farm |
| withig | OE | a willow tree |
| wreyne | ME | twisting, winding, convoluted |
| wrīthan | OE | twisting, winding, convoluted |
| wunden | OE | twisting, winding (of a stream) |

# Index

63